Learning for Ministry

Learning for Ministry

Making the most of study and training

Steven Croft and Roger Walton

CHURCH HOUSE
PUBLISHING

Church House Publishing
Church House
Great Smith Street
London SW1P 3NZ

Tel: 020 7898 1451
Fax: 020 7898 1449

ISBN: 978-0-7151-4278-3

Published 2005 by Church House Publishing in
collaboration with Methodist Publishing House

The opinions expressed in this book are those of
the individual authors and do not necessarily
reflect the official policy of the General Synod or
The Archbishops' Council of the Church of England.

Printed in England by The Cromwell Press,
Trowbridge, Wiltshire

Contents

Preface

Learning for Ministry is designed as a simple handbook for all those who are beginning the journey of preparing for recognized ministries in the Church.

We have in mind particularly people beginning a course of training for licensed lay ministry or ordained ministry in the Methodist Church or the Church of England. We hope the book may be useful to those in similar positions in other Churches.

The book has grown out of our experience of working with many different people who are beginning this journey. For five years we worked closely together within St John's College, Durham, where Steven was Warden of Cranmer Hall (the Anglican theological college there), and Roger is still Director of the Wesley Study Centre (the Methodist training establishment).

Before Roger became Director of the Wesley Study Centre, he headed up the Open Learning Centre for the Methodist Church and has been a Methodist minister for 25 years. Steven was in parish ministry for 13 years before becoming Warden of Cranmer Hall in 1996. In 2004 he took up a new appointment as Archbishops' Missioner and leader of Fresh Expressions, encouraging new expressions of church life across the Church of England and the Methodist Church.

We hope that this book will be a useful companion as advance reading and through the first year or so of your course. Most of the chapters are very basic and introductory and require no initial background knowledge. A few are more demanding and may mean more when you are part-way into your course rather than at the very beginning. You don't have to start at the beginning and work your way through to the end.

We also hope that the book will be a helpful companion and guide to the very large number of people who are called to share the ministry of preparing others in colleges, courses and schemes, as teachers and tutors.

The book grows out of five years of working closely together on a daily basis and of many conversations with colleagues on particular issues in theological education and training. We have each taken responsibility for particular chapters and revised one another's work. Where we have included personal examples (an essential part in helping learning for ministry in our view) we have let you know who is speaking. Overall, we both 'own' what is said throughout the book.

As much as possible, we have tried to write for all kinds of training contexts and have offered the work for comment to those who are more experienced in courses, schemes and lay training.

Working with those who are preparing for ministry is a great privilege and itself forms a rich learning environment. We would like to acknowledge and say thank you for what we have learned over many years of working with colleagues and from what has been shared with us by students. Insight has often come through people sharing what has not been working for them in the training process as well as what has been helpful. A final thank you is reserved for our two families who generously tolerate a commitment to writing in the midst of the other demands of life.

Roger Walton

Steven Croft

1

Making a map

We hope that this book will be a useful guide book for people preparing for Christian ministry which is in some way recognized and authorized in the life of the Churches. The book is therefore for those who are exploring a call to ordination or beginning training; those starting out as local preachers or in Reader ministry; those who are learning new pastoral skills or preparing to be evangelists and church planters. It is intended for anyone who is beginning that kind of preparation. We, the authors, have used the term 'minister' throughout the book to refer to all of these different ways of serving God in the life of the Church. When we refer specifically to a minister who is ordained, we will use the terms deacon, presbyteral minister (for Methodists) or priest (for Anglicans).

This first chapter is a kind of map – an overview – of the whole book and explains the different elements in preparation and how they fit together. In any preparation, it is important to be clear about expectations.

A simple overview

There are many different ways of describing the process of preparing for ministry. In this book, we suggest that you think of it in four interlinked parts:

- Knowing God better;
- Knowing yourself better and being changed;
- Understanding and serving the Church;
- Understanding and caring for God's world.

Although, perhaps, hard to measure, a good test of any course is whether you can get to the end and say that you have moved on in each of these areas. If you take away any of the four, it ought to be obvious that something is missing in your preparation for ministry even if you don't know what it is. Getting the foundations right is partly about understanding these different elements of preparing for ministry and getting them in the right balance.

This book falls into four Parts, corresponding with these four elements of preparation. We have also included a fifth Part about how different people learn best in different ways.

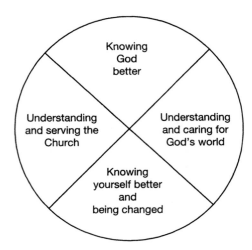

This chapter gives an overview of all four Parts dealing with the elements of preparation and ends with some of our assumptions about the process of learning about ministry which we hope you'll find helpful as you start out.

Knowing God better

Pause for thought

Take a few moments to write down some of the things you are sure of about God. How did you come to know them?

How did you come to know God?

How do people get to know God better?

Part of all ministry is helping people to know God better.

For that reason, part of all preparation for ministry is to help those in training themselves to come to know God better. This is a very bold aim. There are certainly many ways of studying religious things which are not at all about knowing God. A student who goes to a university to take a degree in theology or religious studies may not look to know God any better at the end of the course than at the beginning. They may not even believe in God or they may be a follower of another faith. But at the heart of preparing for Christian ministry has always been a strong sense that we study and learn in order to know God better.

For that reason, all preparation for ministry is grounded in worship and prayer: encountering God particularly in the Scriptures and in the sacraments. All

Check it out

In Mark's Gospel, Jesus calls the twelve disciples 'to be with him and to be sent out'. (Mark 3.14)

preparation for ministry has some element of community as part of our growing. One of the ways we share together is in common worship. You should expect to encounter different traditions and different ways of offering worship. One of the reasons for this is to help you to know God better. In a similar way, at the heart of your preparation for ministry, there will be ways to help you grow in your own life of personal prayer (see Chapter 2). The context for your preparation will be common worship and your own personal life of prayer.

In addition to sharing in common worship and growing in your personal prayer life, your studies will take you deeper into three areas which help Christians grow in their knowledge of God.

The Bible

The first is through the Scriptures. Preparation for all ministry always means engaging in a deeper way with the Bible. This will mean in turn thinking about ways to study and understand the Old and the New Testaments. It may involve some study of biblical languages and history in order to understand the Bible better in its context. It will mean close study of the text and comparing one part of the Bible with another to build a clear picture. It will mean thinking through what makes for responsible and careful interpretation of Scripture today. The biblical courses you study may cover areas such as:

- Old Testament introduction; New Testament introduction – general overviews of the Bible;

- Hebrew; Greek – the original biblical languages;

- Particular texts (such as John's Gospel or the Psalms);

- Understanding and using the Scriptures (also called 'hermeneutics').

The amount of biblical study in your own course may depend on the ministry for which you are preparing. If this is to include public teaching and preaching, then expect a significant proportion of your course to be about the Bible. You will be spending many years helping people know God better through the way you use Scripture. There is more about beginning biblical study in Chapter 3.

Thinking about worship and prayer

Most forms of Christian ministry will involve helping to plan and lead worship both on Sundays and on special occasions. Most forms of Christian ministry will also involve helping other people to pray. Examples might include leading a confirmation class, leading a school assembly, taking a funeral, leading Sunday morning worship, or praying with someone who is dying. Your preparation for ministry will involve some form of engagement with worship and prayer (*doing it*). It will also mean, however, that you need *to think and to learn* about worship and prayer in all kinds of ways and to practise leading worship with feedback from others. The actual study of worship will include:

- Spirituality: looking at the different ways Christians pray;

- Worship (or liturgy): the development of different styles of worship and ways in which they are used today;

- The Sacraments: understanding in particular the great sacraments of baptism and Holy Communion.

> **Liturgy** is the term used in church life to describe the carefully composed words and frameworks we use in church services, some of which are written down in authorized prayer books. The word means, literally, 'work of the people', because worship is the most important task of the people of God.

> An old and helpful definition of a **sacrament** is 'an outward and visible sign of an inward and invisible grace'. Most Churches believe in and practise the two sacraments explicitly commanded by Jesus (baptism and communion). Some traditions give five other special actions the status of sacrament: marriage, ordination, confirmation, anointing for healing and anointing before death.

Thinking about the Christian tradition

It is easy to forget that Christians today benefit from a rich heritage. We are not the first generation of Christians. Many others have gone before us. Each generation has wrestled with questions of living, understanding and communicating faith in their own times. There is a long story to tell and to learn of God's people throughout the world and over thousands of years. Vital parts of that story include the way in which the early generations of the Church struggled to clarify the heart of Christian belief in the great creeds; the way in which Christians have (sadly) separated from one another because of their different understandings of truth; the way in which the good news spread throughout the whole world; the beginnings of the different Churches we know today as Anglican and Methodist; movements of renewal and fresh understanding (such as the great recovery of the ministry of the whole people of God in recent years).

It is not easy to be a Christian in Britain at the beginning of the twenty-first century. Much of our culture has become indifferent or even hostile to Christian values. For that reason, those who are to offer public Christian ministry need to push down very deep roots not only into the Bible but into the story of the Church. The more uncertain the times we live in, the more we need to know who we are as the people of God and the movements which have shaped our history.

This way of understanding the tradition helps us to know God better as we think about how Jesus is fully human and fully God (for example) or about how we understand the relationship between Father, Son and Holy Spirit. There is an overlap here, because study in these ways also helps us to understand ourselves (where we have come from), the Church (how it is formed) and, at least in part, God's world. For that reason, the areas of study where we recover and study our own tradition have a particular importance. They will include:

- The study of what Christians believe (sometimes called doctrine, systematic theology or even just theology);

- The study of Church history – either in overview or looking at particular themes or periods;

- Close study of the beliefs of our own Churches, including foundation documents (such as *The Book of Common Prayer*, or the sermons and letters of John Wesley).

Doctrine means 'teaching'. Normally courses on doctrine look at the teaching and belief of the Church covered in the creeds.

Theology means simply orderly and rational conversation about God.

Systematic theology is about drawing together our different beliefs and understanding about God into one complete whole or 'system'.

Knowing yourself better and being changed

It may seem a strange thing at first to realize that one of the main subjects you will study is yourself. When people train to be car mechanics or driving instructors their course will include very little focus on themselves. Some people who begin preparing for ministry with you will know themselves very well already – perhaps you will fall into that category. Other people will not have done very much thinking about this area of training at all. It may all seem strange and slightly disturbing.

Why is getting to know yourself so important as part of preparing for ministry? Here are three reasons.

The first is about Jesus. The whole of Christian faith centres around the truth that God became a human person. The richest and deepest way God communicates with the world is through the Son. Jesus, in turn, becomes the pattern for all Christian ministry. Whatever we do, it is the person we are which shapes our ministry – far more than the knowledge we possess or the skills we have. When Paul gives his great address to the elders of Ephesus, he asks them to take as their model, first and foremost, the way that he lived and only then his teaching.

Check it out

Read the whole speech in Acts 20.17-38. It is one of the foundation texts in the New Testament for understanding Christian ministry and one of the most moving scenes in Acts. For a different way of confirming the same truth read 1 Corinthians 13.

This means, in preparing for ministry you will need to pay great attention to who you are: to your integrity of life; to your maturity (both strengths and weaknesses); to your gifts; to your lifestyle; to the ways in which you relate to others. The deep and long Christian tradition about any kind of ministry is that at the heart of what we do is our character. Who we are is, in the end, more important than what we know or the things we can do.

The second reason, which may sound obvious, is that ministry is all about people. To do ministry well, therefore, you need to make every effort to understand people. It is never easy to understand other people. But there is one person you can get to know extremely well: yourself! It makes sense in our development as ministers to make the best use we can of that resource.

And the third reason will already be familiar. All Christian ministry is very difficult and demanding. There are no exceptions. Most of us need to grow up and to grow stronger in order to take on increased responsibility in the Christian community. That means being prepared to take a long look at ourselves, to get to know ourselves better and, where necessary, to be changed.

Formation

You will find that different people use different words to describe the process of preparation for ministry. Some people favour the term *education* which suggests a process similar to a school or a university, where the emphasis is on acquiring knowledge and academic skills.

Some people like the term *training* which suggests a process similar to an apprenticeship for a practical task, where the emphasis is learning on the job and acquiring particular skills.

In recent years, the Church of England and the Methodist Church have favoured the term *formation* as a third term for the process of preparation for ministry. Formation places the emphasis on personal growth and change alongside acquiring new knowledge and new skills. It catches the sense that at the heart of preparation and learning for ministry is our growth and development as people.

How do we get to know ourselves better?

Some of the ways we get to know ourselves better in formation for ministry are:

- Reflecting on our story so far in conversation and in writing;
- Becoming part of new communities;
- Being taken outside familiar environments and reacting to new things;
- Thinking about particular incidents or trends with a tutor or support group;
- Working to bring together our understanding of faith and ministry with the person God is calling us to be.

You will find out more about this kind of learning in Chapters 6, 8 and 10.

Pause for thought

How would you describe yourself to someone you have never met?

Make a list of what you think are your best qualities.

Think of an event or experience which helped you learn about yourself.

Understanding and serving God's people, the Church

All recognized and authorized ministry has something to do with the service in or on behalf of the Church. Different ministers serve the Church in different ways. A pastoral assistant or cell group leader within a large congregation will mainly be concerned with their own situation but will still benefit from a much broader and deeper perspective on what the Church is called to be. A recognized evangelist may find herself working for a group of churches across a circuit or a deanery. That is likely to call for a broader understanding of church life and a range of different traditions. A deacon is likely to be working at the margins and boundaries of church life helping the Church to serve its local community: he will still need some understanding of what the Church is called to be and how it operates. A stipendiary priest or minister will normally find herself serving and helping to lead several local communities with different stories, different traditions and (possibly) different pictures of the future.

An important part of all formation for ministry is deepening and extending your understanding and experience of the life of the Church. This should be happening in at least two ways.

First, your preparation for ministry will be designed so that students gain an increased vision and understanding of what the Church is called to become. It is absolutely vital that this vision is nurtured, stretched, challenged and built up through all of your preparation for ministry. This happens through study (as you reflect on the biblical tradition and on the Church down the ages) and through practical placements in a range of different situations which help you see different elements in what the Church is called to be. Unless this vision is nurtured and built up as in preparation for ministry, you may bring very little that is new to the Churches in the future.

> The Greek word for church is *ekklesia*. The word used for our understanding of what the Church is called to be is **ecclesiology**. It means simply orderly and rational conversation about the Church.

Alongside this nurturing of what the Church is called to become, those in training also have opportunity to get to know the Church as it actually is in different ways. This will certainly involve placements of different kinds (often followed by some kind of reflection). It will involve getting to know the different people on the course who will have very different experiences of church life. It may involve spending time in churches of different traditions or different denominations. You will also discover new things about the life of the Church as you look at Church history; as you have opportunity to study the worldwide Church; as you use statistics and trends to think about what is happening in the life of the Church in the present day. As well as all of this, there will be many elements in your course which equip you in different areas of ministry which are intended to build up the life of God's people for service in the whole of society.

Courses where those in training engage with these issues may include:

- Looking at the roots of the Anglican and Methodist traditions or at the ecumenical movement;

- Evangelism, nurture and Christian education;

- Preaching;

- Pastoral care;

- Learning about fresh expressions of church and church planting;

- Different forms of congregational studies.

Check it out

Read Ephesians 4.1-16 – another great New Testament passage on ministry. Different ministries are given by God to the Church 'to equip the saints' and bring God's people to maturity.

Watch out for tension!

As you try and think on the one hand about what the Church is called to be and on the other hand about what the Church is actually like, you will probably find there is some distance between the two! The gap may actually seem to become much wider as you begin serious preparation for ministry. This is a very important tension to hold in your thinking. Out of this tension will come, in time, new vision for the churches you serve and new energy for your ministry. If ever you lose this tension, you will lose a vital element in your calling.

However, this awareness of a tension between what the Church is and what the Church is called to be, must be held alongside the calling of every minister to love the Church, and trust that God is at work renewing his own people. Too much tension with too little love produces ministers who are cynical. Too little tension alongside love for the Church produces ministers who have no vision for change and growth and who become complacent. Tension and love combine in

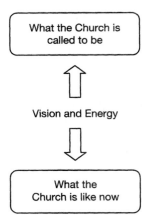

ministers who are called to love the Church into new possibilities and a new effectiveness in its service of God's kingdom.

Learning about ministry and thinking about vocation

Preparing for ministry must also include learning and thinking about the nature of the ministry you are called to exercise. Most preparation now begins part-way through the process of discernment of vocation: in other words you enter this process of formation with some idea of how you may be called to serve God but also with a degree of openness as to whether that idea is appropriate and whether it will be confirmed by the Church you are offering to serve.

From earliest times, discernment of vocation has been a matter of balancing individual gifts and a sense of calling, the insights of the local Christian community and those of the wider Church. As part of your own commitment to that process of discernment, there will need to be careful study and deepening of your understanding of a deacon or Reader's ministry (for example) as well as a continued commitment to share in the Churches' process of discernment.

Understanding and caring for God's world

According to one of the best-known verses in the Bible, 'God so loved *the world* that he gave his only Son, so that everyone who believes in him may not perish but have eternal life' (John 3.16). God's love is not limited to the Church but for the whole of creation. Ministry is not simply about serving the Church. Ministry is about sharing in God's love for the world.

The word which sums up God's love for the world is mission. It comes from the Latin word meaning 'to send'. The Father *sends* the Son. The Father and the Son *send* the Spirit. God's mission of love is to establish his just and gracious kingdom in all the earth. The calling of the Church is to share in God's mission to the whole world. Like the disciples in Acts, we are sent to proclaim the good news.

Check it out

Look up some of these key passages on God's mission to the whole world:

- **Genesis 12.1-3**
- **Isaiah 11.1-9**
- **Luke 4.14-21**
- **Matthew 28.16-20**

In order to love the world for God's sake, we must seek to know and to understand the world in which we live. In order to help the Church to live and to serve God's mission, we need to understand the context in which the Church finds itself. This is true whether we are seeking to help young people in our communities; work for justice on behalf of the poor in our city; or support mission partners on the other side of the world.

Learning about the world as part of our formation for ministry will again be a mix of reflecting on our own experiences and more formal learning. It will mean being introduced to and using some of the human sciences: disciplines which have been developed in the last hundred years or so to help people understand an increasingly complex world. Your engagement with this kind of learning is likely to include at least the insights of sociology (the study of society) and psychology (the study of human behaviour and development). You may also need to learn some of the skills of geography (to understand a large city or a rural community), of economics (to gain an insight into global poverty or regeneration), or of the management disciplines (so as to learn how organizations work and what makes for effective leadership). We live in a multi-faith society in a multi-faith world: some understanding of other faiths is therefore vital to understand and care for our neighbours. Most of us live in a changing and complex culture where we find ourselves attempting to communicate Christian faith to those whose values and patterns of thinking are very different from our own. For those reasons we need to learn ways of listening to and understanding culture and shaping our message so it can be heard well.

Areas of your study which will engage with these things will include:

- Ethics: how Christians live and speak to society in a changing world;

- The study of other religious communities and those with no faith;

- Apologetics: defending and commending Christian faith;

- Psychology, sociology and other human sciences;

- Communication through a variety of media.

A particular (and difficult) discipline to master is the bringing together of the understanding we gain from this thinking about the world around us with the insights we gain from Scripture and the Christian tradition. How do people learn to think in a Christian way about the range of complex questions which confront any Christian minister today, listening both the insights of faith and to the experience of the people around us? This discipline of learning how to bring these insights together is absolutely vital for ministry. It is called by different names in different forms of training: practical theology; theological reflection; pastoral theology or the pastoral cycle. At its heart is learning ways of thinking which are essential to equip us to minister in a rapidly changing world.

Pause for thought

You are bringing with you into formation a range of different skills and experiences and a particular perspective of the world.

Which are the most important insights and qualities?

How did you learn them?

Summary

There are four elements in any process of learning about ministry, summarized in the diagram opposite. Most of the different parts of your formation will contribute to one or more of these four elements.

Overall, there is a lot to learn, but here are two things to encourage you:

- You don't have to learn everything at once or even in the next couple of years. Formation and learning for ministry will continue over a whole lifetime.

- You are already bringing with you a great deal of understanding in each of these four areas. See this as a foundation on which you can build in this next stage of your journey.

Going further

At the end of every chapter we have included some ideas, questions and exercises for you to think about: on your own, as part of a small group or in conversation with a guide or tutor. At the end of most chapters (but not here) there are also some ideas for further reading.

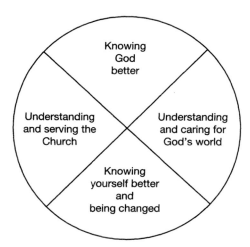

1. Look again at the four areas of learning which are part of formation for ministry. Which is the most important for you? Which is the least important? Which do you look forward to the most? Which the least?

2. Explain the difference between the terms *education, training* and *formation.*

3. For each area of learning, make a list of three lessons you have learned (about God, about the Church, about yourself and about the world) that you want to bring with you into the next part of the journey.

4. If you haven't done so already, find out as much as you can about the overall process of discernment and vocation you will follow. How well does it fit with the process described here?

5. Look at the different elements in your formation over the next year. Can you relate each one to one or more of these four elements?

Part One: Knowing God better

2

Worship and prayer

At the heart of formation for ministry is knowing God. At the heart of knowing God is the deepening of our life of worship and prayer. Therefore somewhere at the heart of preparing for ministry is growing in our experience of these areas of the Christian life.

Mark's Gospel uses a powerful phrase to describe what was in the mind of Jesus when he called the twelve disciples. They were called 'to be with him and to be sent out' (Mark 3.14). The phrase is a helpful summary for the life of a disciple in any generation: we are called into this rhythm of being with Jesus and being sent out. It is the deep rhythm of worship and mission which is the heartbeat at the centre of the Christian way. The same rhythm is there in Jesus' summary of the law: 'love the Lord your God with all your heart, and with all your soul, and with all your mind, and with all your strength . . . love your neighbour as yourself' (Mark 12.29-31).

Those called to ministry in the life of the Church in the present day are therefore called, with every disciple, to be with Jesus and to be sent out. This means that we are called to set worship and prayer at the heart of our lives, following the example of Jesus and the apostles and those who have gone before us as ministers of the gospel. However we may be called to serve God, it is vital that our lives are centred on this call to worship and prayer. Lay preachers and Readers, those called to plant new churches, youth leaders and evangelists need to attend to this area of their lives just as much as full-time ministers and bishops.

Check it out

Look up the references to Jesus at prayer at key moments in the Gospels:

- Mark 1.35
- Luke 5.16

And these references where Jesus is teaching about prayer:

- Mark 11.22-24
- Matthew 6.5-15
- Luke 11.1-13

This may sound a very obvious place to begin to think about formation. However, one of the odd things about a period of preparation for ministry is that, in reality, people find that time for worship and prayer is continually pushed to the edges of their time and energy. If you have a weekend on your course or a summer school – or even if you are training full-time – there seem to be so many other things to do and, strange though it may seem, it becomes hard to find quality time for worship and prayer. During a time of formation there will be many things competing for your attention: books to read; essays to write; a new community to get to know; juggling of family and work responsibilities; placement commitments to fulfil. It becomes surprisingly easy for worship and prayer to be squeezed out. We soon find ourselves complaining, like Martha, that there is so much work to do. We need to hear Jesus' word to her as life-giving and life-saving: 'Martha, Martha, you are worried and distracted by many things; there is need of only one thing' (Luke 10.41). The context of the story makes it clear that the 'one thing' needed is to sit at the Lord's feet and listen to what Jesus is saying. The same principle holds true in every period of our lives: if we put prayer and worship in the last place, not setting aside time but leaving it, as it were, to when we have some time and some energy, we will not grow very much in our relationship with God. If we try and set prayer and worship in first place, whatever our life circumstances, and then allocate time to other things, the chances are that we will continue to grow and mature in this most important of relationships. In one sense, the most important decision you will make in your process of formation is this one.

Some people fall into the trap of putting off giving more time to prayer and worship until their period of learning is over, life is more 'settled' and they have more time to give to ministry (particularly if that ministry is going to be stipendiary). Again, it may surprise you to learn that in all forms of ministry, the same thing happens: worship and prayer keep on slipping towards the edge of people's time and energy.

> A survey of ministers across denominations in the 1990s found that the average stipendiary minister worked 60 hours a week and spent an average of 22 hours a week on administration. A total of 38 minutes was given to personal prayer. That's 5 minutes and 43 seconds a day.

Get some help!

Establishing good spiritual disciplines is very hard work and, for most of us, it doesn't happen overnight. Generally speaking, it is as hard to build up a good habit as it is to get rid of a bad one. If you have ever tried to give up smoking or change your diet or build exercise into your lifestyle, you will know something of what it is like to establish good and helpful patterns of worship and prayer. We need to be patient with ourselves, find patterns that work for us (mostly by trial and error) and persevere.

Most of us need help in this area most of the time in different ways. You will discover as you begin a process of formation, that every person in ministry (or preparation for ministry) needs a support team. One of the first people to put in place in your team is a conversation partner about your life of worship and prayer. Different Christian traditions have different names for such a person. *Spiritual director* is the most common (and the phrase we use here). *Soul friend* is another. *Prayer coach* could be a third. Those responsible for your training should be able to put you in touch with someone who is experienced in this ministry. The relationship needs to be a confidential one and you need to have confidence in speaking about this very personal area of your life (which will only come slowly). Things also need to make sense practically so that the distances are not too great and there is a realistic chance that you can meet at a time convenient to both of you.

The normal pattern for finding a spiritual director is to set up an initial meeting to establish on both sides whether you think that the relationship might work. You then agree together a sensible pattern for meeting. Every two to three months seems about right for most people – perhaps more often at the beginning and in times of transition. An hour is about the right length for the meeting. There is no right or wrong pattern for the conversation but it would normally include a review of how your life of worship and prayer has gone over the last period of time, including mentioning any particular sources of joy and fruitfulness and any particular difficulties. An experienced spiritual director may suggest ways of going further or deeper in prayer from time to time – or they may discern on another occasion that you are trying too hard and need to be more relaxed about your prayers. A good spiritual director will also take the trouble to review all the different elements in this part of your life over time and, possibly, introduce you to new ways of praying and different traditions.

Generally speaking, continuity is a good thing in a relationship with a spiritual director. If you already have someone supporting you in this way, it is normally a good idea to continue with that relationship as you begin a new period of preparation for ministry (providing you are not moving a long distance away). However, there are also moments of key change and growth in your life where a fresh voice can bring a new perspective.

Learn to talk to yourself

A second key element in growing in your life of prayer is to have the courage to reflect on how your spiritual journey is going from time to time. One of the best tried-and-tested ways to do this is to begin keeping a spiritual journal. The only things you need are a notebook, something to write with and a bit of time and space. You may want to write down in your journal your hopes and fears about this part of your formation. You may want to record particular joys or consolations in prayer and also any difficult experiences. It may be helpful to make a note of any particular Scripture verses or other words which are challenging or encouraging. Over time a journal builds into a way of having a conversation with yourself, of working through problems, of communing with your soul (to use the language of the Psalms). You may not often have a reason to read back over what you have written, but on the occasions you do it may be possible to see recurring patterns and gain new insight into your spiritual life over time.

In case you want to begin straight away, here is an exercise to get you started.

Pause for thought

Try to think of five different things which have sustained you spiritually over the last period of your life and the ways in which you have worshipped God and prayed.

Examples might include a pattern of Bible reading; worship in a particular style; an annual retreat or Christian festival; praying with a spouse or close friends; time alone while walking the dog.

How do you anticipate changes in the next year may affect these elements of your spirituality?

Common worship

An old catechism begins like this:

Q: What is the chief end of man?

A: The chief end of man is to know God and enjoy him for ever.

Our main activity in heaven will be worship. Our primary calling on earth is worship: the praise of God. If we are called to recognized ministry in the life of the Church, a large part of what we do may be about helping others to worship in different ways.

> A **catechism** is a summary of Christian belief for the purpose of teaching the faith to children and new Christians. Traditionally, a catechism is in a question and answer form and learned by heart. This is the beginning of the Westminster Catechism, written in 1647.

Changing patterns

Your own patterns of public worship are likely to change as you begin a process of formation for ministry. Worship on Sundays with God's people in church will remain central to your calling. However, you may also find that Sunday services are increasingly a time when you give attention to your own contribution to worship. If you are on placement, learning to lead services or preach for the first time, it can be difficult to focus in the same way on praising God. You may also become more aware of the mechanics of the service or more critical of the way things are done as you grow in your experience of ministry. These are natural and understandable developments but they can also be distracting from the main purpose of worship, which is the praise of God. If you are preparing for a long period of recognized ministry, you will need to be able to grow to the point where you are able both to worship God and share in leading the service. Normally, you will only reach this point when all the mechanics of the service are second nature. However, even at the beginning of this journey it is helpful to keep the following points in mind:

- Try to remember that the primary reason you have come to church is to worship God, and only secondarily to contribute to the service or be prepared for ministry.

- Be diligent and careful in your preparation so that you are not distracted during worship by things you should have done several days before.

- Arrive in good time for the service so that you have at least some time for your own personal prayers and to remember why you have come before engaging with the 'work' of the service.

- Take some time after the service and before you go home to give thanks to God for all his grace and to offer your own contribution back to him.

In any process of formation, time will also be given to prayer and worship with the community which makes up your course or college or training scheme. Here, as in churches where you are on placement, you may encounter unfamiliar practices or services. If you come across things you don't understand, ask for an explanation. If you meet things you don't immediately agree with, find out more and feel free to disagree. Christians do not all see things the same way. Part of the learning in a community of formation comes from dialogue about differences. If you are a Methodist student preparing for ministry in a predominantly Anglican course or college (a more common experience than the other way round) then there may be much about the culture of worship which seems different and difficult. Learn what you can but don't be afraid to seek to challenge and to change what is there.

You will almost certainly have the opportunity to contribute to and to shape the worship offered by your community of formation. Again, do all you can to share something of yourself. Treat the opportunities for worship together with a wide range of committed Christian disciples and ministers in training for what they are: a great privilege and a wonderful opportunity for learning and for growth.

The Daily Office

From earliest times, Christians living and praying in community have needed to develop a balanced framework for common daily prayer to ensure that the community and individuals receive the right spiritual diet. Just as a local church needs to reflect on its Sunday worship (the music style, the balance of services, the length of the sermon), so a community of ministers in formation needs to reflect on its own pattern of regular shared prayer. This reflection will be just as much of a priority in a course where the time together is spread over a year in evenings, Saturdays or weekend residentials as it is in a college with a pattern of alternating terms and vacations.

Patterns of regular prayer together have their roots in the pattern of prayer used by Jesus and his disciples (which was related in some way to the daily prayer of the synagogue and the temple) and which was continued by the first communities of Christians (Acts 2.42-47).

From the fourth century onwards, Christians began to live together in monastic communities in order to be able to give more time to worship and prayer. At the heart of the monastic rule of life is the saying or singing of what is called the Daily Office. In the Benedictine tradition (the most influential), the community gathers together for prayer seven times a day. The prayers are focused around the praise of God, attending to Scripture and intercession for the Church and the world.

This monastic tradition has influenced patterns of prayer developed by and for the clergy (and hence all in recognized ministries). In the English Reformation,

> The **Reformation** is the name given to a series of changes in the life of the Church in Europe in the sixteenth century (the 1500s). The great Protestant traditions separated from the Roman Catholic Church. Thomas Cranmer was Archbishop of Canterbury during the English Reformation and the principal author of *The Book of Common Prayer* – an important document for both Anglicans and Methodists.

Thomas Cranmer reduced the number of Offices each day to two: Morning and Evening Prayer. These were to be said by all clergy in their parish church as an offering of public worship. The Offices still have at their heart the offering of praise to God; attending to the public reading of Scripture and intercession for the Church and for the world. One of Cranmer's chief concerns was to make sure both clergy and people knew the Scriptures. *The Book of Common Prayer* contains a lectionary (or tables of Scripture readings) setting out which lessons should be read on every day. In the course of a year, the book of Psalms is read every month, the Old Testament is read once, and the New Testament is read twice.

Those ordained in the Church of England are still required to say the Daily Office as the heart of their own work of prayer and follow a set pattern of readings (though one which is less demanding in terms of the quantity of Scripture). In many places (but not all) the times of the Office are made known in the parish church. The common life of the Church of England is governed and shaped by Canon law. Canon C 26 reads:

> Every bishop, priest and deacon is under obligation, not being let by sickness or other urgent cause, to say daily the Morning and Evening Prayer, either privately or openly; and to celebrate the Holy Communion, or be present thereat, on all Sundays and other principal Feast Days. He is also to be diligent in daily prayer and intercession, in examination of his conscience, and in the study of the Holy Scriptures and such other studies as pertain to his ministerial duties.

Clearly these guidelines do not apply in the same way to recognized lay ministers in the Church of England. However, there is undoubtedly an expectation that those called to such ministries will pay attention to their life of prayer.

The Church of England has recently revised the Daily Office and the final version was published in 2005 as *Common Worship: Daily Prayer*. The book provides:

- Several ways of praying, from a very simple shape for Prayer During the Day to a full Morning and Evening Prayer;

- Seasonal variations for the form and content of daily prayer;

- Resources for praise and for intercessions;

- Helpful guidelines for individuals and communities.

If you intend to use *Common Worship: Daily Prayer*, you will also need a dated lectionary to help you know what Psalms and readings to follow each day. One of the great advantages of a Daily Office is the sense, even if you are on your own, of praying along with many thousands of other Christians in cathedrals, parish churches and other communities across the world. At the heart of the Office (and of daily prayer for all Christians, there are the same three elements:

- The praise of God;

- Attending to Scripture;

- Intercession for the Church and for the world.

In the Methodist Church there is no single tradition or way of praying individually or together but many helpful insights and resources. Methodists therefore have greater freedom than Anglicans in developing their own patterns of prayer, but all would seek to keep these three principles at the heart of a daily discipline. *The Methodist Worship Book* contains a simple outline for daily Morning and Evening Prayers, and the Methodist Church centrally provides a daily guide for intercession. Of widespread use among Methodists is the annual *Methodist Prayer Handbook*, which offers a variety of prayers for daily use, a focus for intercessions for each of the months, and a lectionary of readings for the year. Many in ministry develop a pattern of using this both for private devotions and shared times of prayer with other.

Different streams and traditions of church life have developed which are shaped around different priorities in personal prayer. For some, a daily sharing in the Eucharist is a very important part of their spirituality and formation. Others have been nurtured in the long evangelical tradition of the quiet time with its emphasis on careful reading of Scripture, often with the help of dated Bible reading notes or commentaries, and on personal intercession. Still others are formed by a more contemplative tradition with space simply to be still before God. Whatever your journey this far, it is very important both to value and cherish what has helped you to grow in your love of God and to continue to be open to new insights and possibilities.

Shaping intercession

A particular part of a minister's calling is to pray for the kingdom to come and, especially, to pray for other people: for their well-being, conversion to faith, discipleship and ministry. This may be something which has been a significant part of your own life thus far. You may have learned how to fulfil this ministry as an element in your own growth in faith from others who have prayed for you. However, at least some people beginning a process of formation have very little experience of praying for others and will need to develop and grow in this discipline.

Pause for thought

A simple way to begin is to make a list in a small notebook of those for whom you feel you have a responsibility to pray regularly. This might include a daily list (for your family and close friends and for urgent needs). It might also, in time, include a weekly list to pray for people for whom you are particularly responsible.

As a vicar (Steven writes), it was my own habit to try to pray through the church electoral roll once each week, dividing it up between the different days. In the college context, I tried to do the same thing with the community of formation. I also have a monthly prayer diary for a different and wider group of people to support and remember them in prayer.

Finding space

An important element in all these aspects of ministry are times of deeper refreshment, challenge and renewal which come through time spent away from the normal rhythms and responsibilities of life in quiet days or residential retreats. Again, this is likely to be a new experience for many as they begin a period of formation. You will need some guidance on how to use these times. This should be provided, but if it is not don't be afraid to ask for some suggestions. It is likely that some of the experiences will be really helpful and give you new things to go on building into your pattern of prayer and the Christian life. Some of them may not be as helpful for you. It is wise simply to accept that and, as it were, move on.

Sometimes a retreat or some other element in your formation may introduce you to a whole new tradition of spirituality or a stream to be followed which proves a rich source of renewal. When that happens, make time to follow this up with your spiritual director and in other reading and opportunities for worship.

Finding your own rhythm

One of the best and wisest pieces of advice given to people learning to pray was given by Ignatius, the founder of the Roman Catholic Jesuit order. One of his key principles was 'use what helps'. We are all very different from each other and we change throughout our lives. Do your best to think about what helps you. In particular, try to learn your own best rhythms for prayer in terms of the time of day (are you a morning or evening person?); your love for and need of either freedom or organization in your prayer life; your own particular gifts in prayer and your weaknesses; and the demands of your own rhythms of life. If you have young children and you lose sleep regularly, the early mornings may not be the best time to pray. If you go through a demanding period in your working life then it is likely that you will not have much energy in your prayers. Most churches and communities of formation have their own rhythm with particularly demanding seasons and also times of the year when there is more space. Do your best to find out what these are. It is also wise not to expect too much of yourself during a time of major change or transition (although this can also create space to build some good new patterns).

God at work!

The process of formation for ministry is more than simply a human process of education, training and personal change. As Christians we believe that our loving God is at work in our lives through the grace and power of the Holy Spirit. God's grace works to draw us to him in a relationship of love. Part of our calling is to ensure that we respond to God's grace through building healthy and helpful patterns of prayer in order to keep this relationship at the centre of our life and ministry. All those involved in formation for ministry need to ensure that growing in our knowledge of God is at the core of all we do.

Going further

1. What would you say to a fellow minister in formation who came out with the following?

   'The worship on the course is more of a hindrance than a help.'

   'Where do I go to really worship!'

   'Sorry I fell asleep in the lecture; I was up at 5.30 for my quiet time!'

   'I can't read the Bible any more without having more questions than answers.'

   'I seem to have lost sight of God in all there is to do.'

2. The idea of a pattern of helpful spiritual disciplines is summarized in the little phrase 'a rule of life'. Agree with yourself (and then possibly with a tutor or spiritual director) what your own 'rule of life' might be in the next year, around the following headings:

   Your normal pattern of Sunday and midweek worship;

   Your normal pattern of daily prayer (both time and content);

   Your pattern of a retreat or quiet days;

Your relationship with a spiritual director;

Your pattern of intercession.

3.   What are the ways in which you have sensed God working in your life or guiding you over the past year?

Further reading

Common Worship: Daily Prayer, Church House Publishing, 2005.

The Methodist Worship Book, Methodist Publishing House, 1999.

The Methodist Prayer Handbook, Methodist Publishing House, annual publication.

Christopher Cocksworth and Jeremy Fletcher, *Common Worship: Daily Prayer*. Grove Worship Series, 166, Grove Books, 2001.

Stephen Cottrell, *Praying Through Life*, Church House Publishing, 1998, second edition 2003. A short and readable introduction to building prayer into daily life.

Richard Foster, *Streams of Living Water*, HarperCollins, 1999. An accessible introduction to the great traditions of Christian spirituality.

Gerard Hughes, *God of Surprises*, Darton, Longman & Todd, 1985. A now classic introduction to Ignatian spirituality.

The Rule of Benedict. A helpful edition is Esther de Waal, *A Life-Giving Way: A Commentary on the Rule of St Benedict*, Geoffrey Chapman, 1995.

3

Engaging with Scripture

The Bible is one of the greatest treasures of the Christian life. In most services to mark the beginning of a new ministry the candidates are invited to affirm their attitude to Scripture. In the Methodist ordination services, the candidates are asked the following questions (among others):

> Do you accept the Holy Scriptures as revealing all things necessary for salvation through Jesus Christ our Lord?

> Will you be faithful in worship, in prayer, in the reading of the Holy Scriptures, and in those studies which will equip you for your ministry?

Anglican ordinands and candidates for Reader ministry are asked almost identical questions. The questions echo and draw on Article VI of the Articles of Religion of 1562, the most ancient and authoritative description of Anglican beliefs:

> Holy Scripture containeth all things necessary to salvation: so that whatsoever is not read therein, nor may be proved thereby, is not to be required of any man, that it should be believed as an article of the Faith, or be thought requisite and necessary for salvation.

The Scriptures have a unique place within the Christian life and therefore within Christian ministry and the life of the minister.

A period of formation for ministry is therefore a very important opportunity to continue in and deepen your understanding of Scripture. This will not, of course, be your first exposure to the Bible. You will have listened to Scripture being read in church, probably studied it for yourself and shared in teaching and reflection. Your studies over the next few years will be a continuation of your Bible study thus far and will probably mark a significant deepening of that study. You may want to take a few moments at this point to think about how you have engaged with Scripture in your Christian life thus far. Make notes in your journal or discuss the questions with a friend.

Pause for thought

What are your earliest memories of reading the Bible or hearing it read?

What part did the Scriptures play in your own coming to faith?

What is your own experience of reading Scripture in recent years?

What do you need to learn about most in biblical study?

The Bible and Christian ministry

From the New Testament period onwards, Scripture has played a key role in Christian ministry. In the book of Acts, the twelve apostles appoint seven other ministers because they see their own calling as to devote themselves 'to prayer and to serving the word' (Acts 6.4). This dual focus on the word and on prayer (especially the sacraments) has always been at the heart of presbyteral or priestly ministry. Paul's advice to Timothy has been passed on and lived out from generation to generation of Christian ministers:

> But as for you, continue in what you have learned and firmly believed, knowing from whom you learned it and how from childhood you have known the sacred writings that are able to instruct you for salvation through faith in Christ Jesus. All scripture is inspired by God and is useful for teaching, for reproof, for correction and for training in righteousness so that everyone who belongs to God may be proficient, equipped for every good work. (2 Timothy 3.14-17)

Acts and Timothy are building here on one of the main streams of the Old Testament tradition that those who are faithful to God need to spend time and energy meditating on God's law (see, e.g., Psalm 1, Psalm 19 and Psalm 119 and Joshua 1.8). This is a discipline which is affirmed throughout the history of the Church in every tradition.

Some of the ways we use the Bible in ministry are very obvious. At the heart of Christian worship is the reading of Scripture and preaching which is scripturally based. An extensive knowledge of the Bible and the ability to use Scripture wisely is therefore essential for those who are called to this ministry. However, the Bible also finds a place in Christian ministry in many other ways. Someone who is called to teach children or young people in school assemblies, Christian camps or holiday clubs or out of school clubs is doing so on the basis of using Scripture well. Many different ministers are involved on a week by week basis with teaching the faith to adults through one of the published courses such as Emmaus, Alpha or Disciple, or through material you prepare yourself. Again, this involves reading and using the Bible. Others are involved in leading Bible studies in the context of small groups.

Pastoral visiting will sometimes involve being asked for wise counsel on the basis of Scripture. Often those acting in a pastoral role on behalf of the Church will be asked hard questions about Christian faith. Sometimes these may be about belief: 'How can there be a God of love in a world of such great suffering?' Sometimes they may be about pastoral practice: 'Our teenage daughter is pregnant and is thinking about an abortion. How can we reconcile this with our faith?'

Jason is a local preacher and involved in the finances of his local circuit. There is a proposal to reduce what the churches give to mission in order to make ends meet in this year's budget. Jason draws what he has learned from his biblical studies about the priority of mission for God's people and makes a passionate plea on the basis of Scripture for retaining or increasing this element of the budget.

Anne is a pastoral visitor working mainly with the bereaved. She has a number of conversations with Rosemary, a lifelong church member whose husband has recently died. Rosemary is unable to find in her own Christian understanding any permission to grieve and lament her loss. She feels bound to focus on the joy and hope of resurrection but is unable to move on. Anne takes her to the lament psalms and shows Rosemary a different pathway to bring her broken heart honestly to God and find healing.

Terry is a youth leader. A number of young people in the church have returned from a Christian camp where they have been given very dogmatic teaching that the second coming of Christ will happen in this generation and the true believers will be suddenly snatched into heaven. Terry sits down with the group to study carefully the passages in the Gospels and Revelation and to bring them to a more balanced understanding.

Even these examples do not begin to exhaust the range of ways ministers find themselves using Scripture in ministry. At the heart of those ways will be personal reflection and study of the Scriptures. It is this regular pattern of study and reflection which gives to the Christian minister, over time, the resources and the authority to speak God's word in the midst of a Church and a society which need to hear good news.

Knowledge or skills?

Some people approach a period of study with the idea that this is a tremendous opportunity to fill up some kind of reservoir for teaching and preaching for the rest of their ministry. If this is your aim, then you will probably be looking for your biblical studies courses to cover large areas of Scripture for your own learning and so you can pass that learning on to others.

However, this will not be the primary aim of your course of study, which is intended in this and other ways to prepare you for a lifetime of reading and using Scripture wisely. Instead, the course will seek to help you build the *essential skills and habits* for this lifelong learning and service. The best kind of biblical study is not therefore about how much of the text you can cover during your period of initial training but about how well you can acquire these key skills to understanding and interpret the Bible for the sake of the Church and for your ministry to the wider community.

There are a number of common problems in the approach to Scripture encountered by people beginning a process of formation. The first is a simple lack of familiarity with the Bible which makes it difficult to move on to learning key skills for biblical study. This may be especially true for those who have become Christians as adults or who have never been part of a church where Bible study is encouraged. The second is (curiously) well-formed and particular habits of biblical study and of seeing Scripture, which also make it hard to be open to new insights and skills. The third is connecting your study of Scripture back to the life of ministry through preaching and teaching and in other ways. This chapter attempts to tackle each of these difficulties in turn. We have tried to be as practical as possible in giving you ideas on where to begin in your own study.

Where do I begin?

Modern printing and publishing disguise the size and complexity of the Bible. The Bible is freely available – you probably own several copies of different translations. It is possible to purchase any number of neatly bound, pocket-sized versions which leads us to think that Scripture is much like any other novel or non-fiction book we can borrow from the library.

People who lived before the invention of the printing press (about 500 years ago) found it much easier to grasp the size and complexity of Scripture as well as its special qualities. Then, most books of the Bible would be a single manuscript either bound as a book (like the Lindisfarne Gospels), or as a parchment scroll. Some of the longer books may have run to several scrolls while the shorter ones would be combined. However, it would have been easy to see at a glance that this was a large, complex collection of writings which may not be that easy to get to know or to understand. One of the great achievements of the Reformation was to make the Scriptures available in the languages of the people – previously they were available only in Latin or in the original Greek and Hebrew. At the English Reformation, the Bible began to be read in English in public for the first time.

As you begin to study the Bible in new ways as part of your formation for ministry, it helps to see (or see again) the complexity of Scripture as a collection of different books which has been passed down to us over many generations. Most courses of study will divide the study of Scripture into Old and New Testament studies. In some, the balance between the two is uneven and the Old Testament is somewhat short-changed (a mistake as the Old Testament is the more complex and unfamiliar part of the Bible for most students and a vital resource).

Tools for understanding the Old Testament

Handbooks and dictionaries

A key foundation for beginning Old Testament studies is gaining *an overview* of this part of Scripture, in the sense both of learning the Old Testament story and knowing how the different books fit into that story. You will need a good Bible handbook as an initial reference book, with maps, charts and introductions to each book and each type of book. A Bible dictionary is another essential part of your toolkit to look up and explore material about places, people or themes. You will also find that you need a concordance which lists the different biblical references to particular words or themes. If you have very little idea about the shape of the Bible story or the shape of biblical history, then it may be helpful to read either a short guide to Old Testament times or else a novel (such as Walter Wangerin's *The Book of God*) which gives a dramatic presentation of some of the main episodes of the biblical story. There has been rapid development in using information technology as a tool in biblical studies in recent years, and many biblical translations and standard reference books are now available on CD-ROM. Suggestions will be given by your course leaders.

Biblical languages

The original Old Testament texts are in Hebrew (with some Aramaic in the books of Daniel and Esther) and the original New Testament texts are in Greek. One of the key questions for all those beginning biblical studies is whether you will have the time, ability and support to learn these biblical languages at this point or in the future. To do that, you will need to be prepared to work hard and will need considerable learning support (there are very few people who can teach themselves biblical languages). To get to the point where you can read the Greek or Hebrew text in the same way as you read an English translation takes many years of study. However, to reach the point where you can use an interlinear version and a Hebrew or Greek dictionary to understand more about a particular passage is a more manageable goal for most students. If you are able to get to this point, it will substantially assist your reading of Scripture for many years to come.

Different disciplines in Old Testament study

Like any academic subject, the study of the Old Testament divides into different disciplines. Study of the *language and the text* probably will not concern you a great deal unless you move on to postgraduate work. You will need to know something about different views of the *history* which underlies the biblical narrative (and its relationship to the text). There is a whole discipline of *archaeology* which has explored the Ancient Near East and unearthed material which is relevant to biblical studies (particularly the Old Testament period). This material includes texts from other civilizations which are similar to the biblical material. Beyond the history and archaeology, the study of the Old Testament has spread into different sub-disciplines which focus on different groups of books:

- The Pentateuch (Genesis, Exodus, Leviticus, Numbers, Deuteronomy);

- Historical books (Joshua to 2 Kings and Chronicles–Ezra–Nehemiah);

- The Prophets;

- Wisdom literature (Proverbs, Job, Ecclesiastes);

- Psalms and other poetry (Lamentations, Song of Songs).

Your studies in the initial period of preparation for ministry are likely to focus on the Pentateuch (especially Genesis and Exodus) and the Prophets, with some introduction to other areas of the Old Testament.

There are some books which do not fit neatly into any of these categories and others which occur in more than one. There are also other collections of literature from the period between the Testaments, in particular the Apocrypha – writings which are present in the Greek version of the Jewish scriptures but not the Hebrew version and which are found in some English Bibles.

Tools for understanding the New Testament

Generally speaking, the New Testament is easier to understand and to study. Most of us are more familiar with at least the gospel stories when we begin. The books are shorter and were all written within – at most – 60 years or so of Jesus' death and resurrection. Once again, the study of the language, the text and the background history is extremely helpful: there is a similar need for a good handbook, an overview of the history and (if you can manage it) a basic understanding of the language and the text.

New Testament studies also divide up into different disciplines. Normally the main divisions are:

- The synoptic Gospels (Matthew, Mark and Luke);

- The Johannine writings (the fourth Gospel, the epistles of John and Revelation);

- The letters of Paul;

- Acts (also linked to Luke's Gospel);

- Other writings (the letter to the Hebrews, letters of Peter and James).

Your studies in initial preparation for ministry are likely to focus on the four Gospels and the letters of Paul. Matthew, Mark and Luke are called the *synoptic* Gospels because they need to be studied together (*synoptic* means 'seen together'). These three Gospels share a common core of text (large sections of the Gospel of Mark). Much of the focus of gospel studies is learning about the relationship between these three Gospels and studying the ways in which each has used a similar tradition in very different ways. One of the really essential tools in gospel studies is a version of these three Gospels called a *synopsis* which sets out the text of Matthew, Mark and Luke in three columns side by side. Paul's letters are the earliest documents in the New Testament and the foundation of early Christian teaching. The normal pattern in initial training is to study one of them in depth (usually Romans or 1 Corinthians) as a way of helping you develop the tools for study of the rest.

Commentaries

Commentaries are detailed studies of particular books of the Bible. They can be very short or run to hundreds of pages. The earliest commentaries on Scripture were written in the first centuries of the early Church. However, many more have been produced in recent years. Anyone called to a regular ministry of teaching and preaching will seek, over time, to build up their range of commentaries and reference books to assist that task.

In building up your library, it is wise not invest in a whole series from a particular publisher or single author, but aim for particular writers or commentaries which you find to be helpful. It is an excellent approach to 'try before you buy' (through libraries). You will probably need to focus in the next few years on areas of Scripture you will study during your course. It is also extremely helpful to begin to build a resource of commentaries on the four Gospels: these are likely to be the focus of your teaching and preaching ministry in most churches because of the way we shape our Sunday lectionary. Be on the lookout for recommendations of good commentaries from course teachers and fellow students. File course reading lists carefully – you may want to come back to them many years later.

Reading with open eyes

Reading the Bible is harder than it seems. All of us bring to the text a particular view on a whole range of issues. These views have been formed in us through our previous life experience and our learning. They act as a pair of spectacles through which we interpret the Scriptures. Part of the discipline of biblical study is being aware of the views that we bring to the text and allowing those views to be challenged in our studies.

As a simple illustration of this, ask yourself how many visitors from the East came to see the infant Jesus and his family after his birth in Bethlehem bringing gifts of gold and frankincense and myrrh. What sort of visitors were they? Most of us have formed the view over many years through looking at Christmas cards and infant nativity plays and crib scenes that, of course, there were three visitors and they were kings. If you have never studied the Bible carefully before, you may also believe that the entire story of Jesus' birth is in all four Gospels. After all, it is the part of the story of Jesus best known to people today.

Have a look now at the beginning of each of the Gospels beginning with John and working backwards. You will see (if you did not know already) that there is no story of the birth of Jesus in John's Gospel. Mark makes no mention of it either. Luke has a story of the birth of Jesus which takes place in Bethlehem, which focuses on Mary, and in which Jesus is born in a stable and is visited by shepherds who have seen a vision of angels. Matthew's story has none of these details (apart from Mary and Joseph and Bethlehem). It is only Matthew who tells us that Jesus was visited by *wise men* (the Greek word is *magi*), but we are not told the number of visitors, only the number of gifts. There are no camels and there would not be a snowflake in sight. The three kings of the carols, cards and nativity plays are one way of interpreting the story – but not the only one.

There are many, many more important ways in which our own preconceptions about what we *think* the Bible says prevent us from seeing what the Bible *actually* says. It is very easy for a Christian nurtured in a charismatic–evangelical tradition to read the book of Acts and take notice of all of the signs and wonders, the miraculous conversions and the emphasis on church growth yet miss entirely the substantial themes of the suffering of the Church and the early Christians and the sharing of wealth. Once these things are pointed out by others, we begin to notice them and we find, often, that they challenge us very deeply. It is also easy to imagine the opposite: a Christian nurtured in the tradition of a strong social gospel to highlight the passages about the sharing of wealth and care of the poor in Acts yet skate over the signs and wonders and the growth of the Church. A person who comes to the text firmly convinced that (according to Scripture) women should not share in the ordained ministry of the Church will find it difficult to pay attention to passages such as Luke 24.1-12 (where the women are first witnesses of the resurrection); or Acts 18.26-28 (where a woman takes the lead in correcting the teaching of a man); or Romans 16 (where women are given the titles deacon, leader and apostle). Jesus himself, echoing the prophets, talks about how hard it is to 'see' and 'hear' God's word. It should come as no surprise to find that this is still the case (and that his words apply to us as well as to others).

Is the Bible completely without error?

One of the most common ideas people bring to the text when they begin a course of training for ministry is the idea that the Bible is not only inspired by God and contains all things necessary for salvation but that the text is completely free of any kind of human error. This idea is known as the doctrine of biblical inerrancy or, more commonly, fundamentalism (although this word can have a broad range of other meanings as well).

It is important to recognize that this particular teaching goes much further than either anything the Bible claims for itself, or that the Church of England and the Methodist Church claim for the Bible. The collection of writings which form Scripture are plainly both a (very wonderful) human creation and (through faith) inspired by the Spirit. Evidence of the Spirit working through ordinary, fallible human beings can be seen in:

- The Bible bearing the hallmarks of different human cultures which help shape the text (such as accepting the world view of the time in the Genesis creation accounts; or the acceptance of polygamy in the Genesis narratives);

- The recording of different versions of the same events with discrepancies between the accounts (as in the books of Kings and Chronicles or some of the gospel accounts);

- The complex evolution of different sources and traditions into the text we have today (such as the book of Isaiah which contains material from several different prophets spanning several centuries);

- Developments in thought from the Old Testament to the New Testament (the New Testament abandons violence and war as a way of bringing about God's will – the view reflected in the book of Joshua);

- Different views on a range of subjects throughout the Bible, and debate between the biblical traditions (such as the debate about the relationship between personal sin and suffering we can see between Proverbs and Job and which continues into the New Testament).

To say that the Bible contains these and other marks of its human creation does not mean that it is any less inspired. At the heart of the Christian faith is the belief that God works through human lives and most of all in and through Jesus Christ.

Much contemporary biblical study is about trying to understand these complex human factors which have led to the development of the text of Scripture in its present form. The goal of this study is to help the Church to listen well to the word of God through the Scriptures and to interpret them responsibly for the flourishing of the Christian community and our wider society. For that reason, it is important for those who enter training to grasp that reading and interpreting the Scriptures is not something done authoritatively by any individual alone, but something we do as a community of faith: we need one another and the different perspectives we each bring.

Challenges to faith

Beginning biblical study as part of formation for ministry can sometimes bring challenges to the faith which has become precious to us. We need courage to look again at the foundations of our own Christian belief and to allow those foundations to be examined and, in some cases, rebuilt. The faith we hold ourselves needs to bear more weight as we offer ministry to others. This means there are appropriate occasions when we need to be challenged by those responsible for our learning and those we learn with.

> In my own case (Steven writes), when I first began to study theology, the challenge was most difficult and painful in this area of biblical study because a particular view of the Bible had been so important in my own faith journey. I found it very difficult for a time to accept the (now) very clear evidence that the Scriptures bear all the hallmarks of human creation (including a range of different perspectives and views which reflect particular cultures). At some points in the journey it was very hard indeed

> to see beyond the human sources of Scripture to hear God's
> voice. I had to learn to read the Bible in a different way:
> preserving the same sense of the priority and authority of
> Scripture as the inspired word of God, but accepting a different
> and richer understanding of the way the texts were formed. I
> exchanged a picture of the Holy Spirit dictating the text word
> for word to Moses, Isaiah and the apostle John for a far less tidy
> picture of different authors working within different faith
> communities; of others sifting, weighing and shaping their
> material; of different perspectives of God's grace and of the Holy
> Spirit working through all of this process, through the
> preservation of the text and through the Church today to lead
> us into truth.

This may not be your journey exactly. However, we will all need those who can
be guides to us in the work of building more secure foundations of understanding
so that we in turn can help others.

Connecting Scripture to life

A Christian minister does not devote a lifetime of study to the Scriptures in
order to become knowledgeable in ancient languages or culture or simply to
become an authority on a particular text. We give our best energies to the study
of the Scriptures in order to be able to offer good news and guidance within
both Church and society. Therefore it important on the journey through initial
training not only to give due attention to the content of Scripture and to listen
well to the text through the different academic disciplines, but also to connect
the text clearly to the experience of the Church and the world in the present
day. Again, a significant part of your own biblical study will focus on the ways in
which you use Scripture in preaching and teaching, in pastoral work and
evangelistic ministry, to shape the Church and to influence society.

Offering guidance and reflection to Church and society on the basis of Scripture
is a serious responsibility. The distilling of the insights of Scripture into wisdom for
living is, once again, a habit and practice formed over many years. As part of your
initial training, you will need to give due time to:

- Using the very best linguistic and critical tools to expose the meaning and
  genesis of the text;

- Attending to the different parts as well as to the whole, to the whole as
  well as to the parts;

- Taking care not simply to prooftext the ideas we might bring;

- Allowing for appropriate development and debate within the tradition, particularly between the Old and New Testaments;

- Being aware of your own concerns and prejudice so that you do not screen out all that is challenging, uncomfortable or contrary to your own interests.

The Bible is an immense source of wisdom for the Christian minister and for Christian ministry. In the strong imagery of Genesis taken up in Isaiah and the parable of the sower, the word of God has life-giving, creative power (Genesis 1; Isaiah 55.10-11; Luke 8.4-15). Each of us called to ministry needs to persevere in our commitment to study and to preach this strong, life-giving and creative word of God.

Going further

1. Which parts of Scripture do you most need to get to know over the next six months? Make a plan for how you will go about this.

2. Do you understand the distinction between the Bible being inspired and the Bible being without error? What challenges to your own faith do you anticipate through biblical studies?

3. How would you begin to use and interpret Scripture wisely for a group who were concerned to:

   - Explore the question of debt relief for the poor;

   - Develop a balanced and healthy lifestyle;

   - Review the response a local church makes to the remarriage of divorced people?

Further reading

The Gospel of Mark

Pat Alexander and David Alexander (eds), *The Lion Handbook to the Bible*, third edition, Lion, 2002.

Richard Briggs, *Reading the Bible Wisely*, SPCK, 2003.

Walter Wangerin, *The Book of God: The Bible as a Novel*, Lion, 1998.

4

Exploring the Christian tradition

The third way in which preparing for ministry seeks to help us to know God better is in the exploration of the Christian tradition. By this we mean studying what Christians have written, said and done in the past and in other parts of the world.

Why should we do this? Why should we spend time and effort hearing, reading and perhaps writing about people who may have lived and died a hundred, five hundred or nineteen hundred years ago? Well, there are many reasons. Here are a few:

- *To understand where we have come from.* Many of the hymns we sing, the creeds and prayers we say, and buildings we worship in were created by Christians who lived before us. We have inherited these. They, in this way, have shaped us and how we think about and worship God. Understanding better how the Nicene Creed came to be written, why Charles Wesley or Thomas Cranmer uses certain words and phrases, and what made our forebears build churches and chapels the way they did, can give us greater insight into their faith and ours.

- *To take our place in the work.* Christian mission is like a relay race. Those who went before us pass the baton on to us. The Greek word that we translate 'tradition' means literally a 'passing or handing on'. Knowing more about how they ran their part of the race – how they coped with difficulties, how they shared the good news and how they sustained themselves – can encourage us for the work to which God is calling us. Some of the stories of earlier Christians are powerful testimony to the grace of God: the life and martyrdom of Polycarp in the second century for example, or the witness of Francis of Assisi, the campaigning of William Wilberforce against slavery, or the courage of the Confessing Church in Germany during the Second World War. Other parts of Christian history are more sobering, for example, the Crusades or some aspects of the missionary movement in the eighteenth and nineteenth centuries. Here we become aware of the mistakes and failures of Christians in the past. But these too can be helpful, for we can recognize in them faulty or inadequate expressions of the gospel. As we take our place in the chain, we can be better equipped for what we have to do.

- *To avoid reinventing the wheel.* One big surprise for many theology students is how many of the debates about faith have happened before. Some of the hard questions about belief – why God allows suffering, how can be Jesus be fully human and divine, how can the death of Jesus change things – have been discussed many times in the past. While we will have to address these and many other questions ourselves in our own day, studying how others have wrestled with them can help.

- *To change things.* Appreciating the witness and struggles of previous generations of Christians means that we can pay due honour to them and learn from them. We do not need to be bound by their approach, however. Learning the Christian tradition can give to us a stronger basis to find news ways of witness and worship appropriate to our age.

Perhaps most important is that we can see recurring patterns of God's grace, love and mercy amidst the faithful witness in history and despite the Church's failings. It is in this extended understanding of how Christians in the past have expressed their faith that we can know God better.

Pause for thought

What individuals or stories from Church history have inspired you?

Are there are any things in Church history or current life that you are ashamed of and or would like to change?

What mistakes have you made in your Christian life and what have you learned from those mistakes?

The size of the task

Exploring the Christian tradition is a massive task. Make no mistake about that. Imagine that you decided to climb Mount Everest. There would be many skills to develop, many months, perhaps years of training and preparation, then there would be the demand of the climb itself with all its particular harsh conditions and personal challenges. It would take a great determination, perseverance, skill and hard work and all this might take up three or four years. When you had got to the top you might, rightly, feel a sense of achievement, but you would also see, as you look at the view, that there are several hundred mountains in the range that you had not yet climbed. The Christian tradition has been built up for over 2,000 years and draws on the Jewish tradition which goes back over 2,000 years before that. There have been millions of Christians participating in its life and, like you, contributing to its tradition. There are huge streams of writings, prayers and creeds, vast numbers and styles of buildings and Christian art and a great array of patterns of mission, styles of worship and types of ministry. The Christian tradition is definitely of the mountain range type. It would be foolish to imagine that one can study all of it, whether your training lasts two years or ten years. Even a lifetime of study would only give you a working knowledge of a fraction of the whole.

What does that mean in any particular course or programme? Inevitably it means that you will only study some parts of the tradition. The selection of what parts of the tradition are tackled will be made by the programme designers. You may have options, but the programme itself will have already been carefully put together so as to make an appropriate diet for the ministry preparation you need to undertake. Our experience over several years of designing and teaching courses in preparation for ministry is that there is always more you would like students to study than you can fit into a timetable and that the hardest part of agreeing a programme between teaching colleagues is deciding what will be left out. Furthermore, designers have to make choices between depth of understanding on the one hand and breadth of knowledge on the other hand. If you spend a long time studying the Reformation, for example, you may become aware of many aspects of the subject but consequently may not have the time to study the early Church, the medieval and modern Church in the same depth.

Therefore, you must see any course as the beginning of an exploration of the Christian tradition that you will need to extend over the whole of your ministry.

As with biblical studies, you also need to develop transferable skills. When studying a particular subject (let's say, the meaning of salvation) you will probably be involved in attending a seminar or lecture, and/or meeting with a tutor, reading, searching for and collecting relevant books and articles and perhaps visiting web sites, making notes for an assignment and organizing your work for presentation in a written or oral form. In the process you should get to know key authors, journals where relevant articles may be found, appropriate databases and search engines and which libraries have helpful material. You will also have learned (if you didn't know already) how to take notes, summarize key points in articles and structure your own work to form an argument or present a case. Once these skills have been developed through one study you can use them to tackle another subject, at a later date, perhaps a subject of your own choosing rather than one given.

Different approaches

How might you study the tradition? There are different ways depending on the nature and structure of your programme.

For about two hundred years the study of theology has been divided into four broad areas:

- *Biblical studies.* This has sometimes been called biblical theology (see Chapter 2).

- *Church history.* This is a form of history in which the Christian Church is a major focus. It is not just the story of the Church through time, but also an understanding of the broader history in which the Church has lived and how the two have related and affected each other. It has often included looking at the creeds and other aspects of theological thinking in the context of their development and because of this has sometimes been called historical theology.

- *Systematic theology,* sometimes called doctrine or dogmatics. As we indicated earlier, systematic theology is concerned with coherent and ordered thinking about belief and often involves looking at the major areas of belief such as God, the Trinity, the person of Christ, the nature of salvation and atonement, the Spirit, the Church, creation and the last things. It may also include a study of significant Christian thinkers such as Origen, Augustine, Aquinas, Luther, Calvin, Thomas Cranmer, Richard Hooker, John Wesley, Karl Barth and Jürgen Moltmann.

- *Practical theology.* This area has been about the study of how belief is expressed in practice and what practice tells us about belief. Often this has been explored through thinking about preaching, liturgy, pastoral care and ethics.

These four areas have often been the organizing structure for programmes of theological study and courses preparing people for ministry. They may be discernable in the programme you are starting. In recent years, however, there have been a number of developments that have challenged this programme structure and offered alternative approaches. For one thing, many subjects have developed into major areas of study. For example, the study of mission which was often taught as part of Church history or practical theology, is now regularly a subject area of its own. Second, many other issues have demanded attention in our age such as gender, mass media and culture and rightly have appeared on the curriculum. This has led to serious debates about what must be included at what stage and what should be left out of any programme. Third, and perhaps most significant, have been the changes in thinking about the nature of knowledge and how people learn and, therefore, about the way one should engage with the many aspects of theology.

Some people learn most effectively when they have a problem to solve or they can see a practical outcome; some will learn most effectively when they are actively involved; while others will learn best when given time to reflect or look at a bigger picture. In other words, people are different. Some will learn better when their immediate concerns and the issues of the world are the starting point for the study of theology. Others will learn much by critically looking at the practices of the Church and its questions concerning mission and service, and this will be a way into studying theology.

Thus it is now common to find courses and programmes that put much emphasis on starting practically. Methodist local preachers often study alongside starting to preach and lead worship, at first under the immediate supervision and guidance of an established preacher, but for much of the time taking responsibility for acts of worship themselves. When they come to studying the Bible or the tradition they are naturally asking questions about worship and preaching. Likewise it is common for those preparing for ordained ministry while in full-time or part-time employment to be encouraged to ask questions about and reflect theologically on their paid employment. In some residential programmes large amounts of time may be devoted to placements, with written work required to demonstrate how the questions of the particular context and ministry relate to theology. All this means that practical theology may be the way in and starting point for the study.

Where to start?

So on some courses you will start with a study of the Scriptures, then Church history and systematic theology, and end by asking such questions as 'What does this mean for preaching?' or 'What should I do about marrying divorced people?' or 'What can I write about human cloning?' In other programmes, you may start with practical situations, such as 'How do I care for a person dying of cancer?' or 'How and why is the Church involved in its local community?' or 'What should I preach about this passage next Sunday?' and then begin to explore what the Bible, Church history and theology have to say. It is not the starting point that matters (though it will influence how you proceed), but that you explore all the resources for theology.

The first thing Jane was required to do on her training course was to spend three weeks with a chaplain in a hospice. She had never been in hospice before and was impressed with the care and sensitivity of the staff for patients and families. While she was there a young couple whose baby son was terminally ill asked if the chaplain would baptize him. Though they did not attend church and were unsure what they believed about God they wanted their child to be baptized before he died. Jane was present at the baptism. When she met with her tutor at the end of the three weeks she had lots of questions about this. He discussed the questions with her, gave a short list of books about baptism and asked her to go and find out as much as she could and write a piece about baptism.

Stephen had almost finished the lecture course about Methodism where he had learned something about the differences between Wesleyan, Primitive and New Connexion Methodist strands. He began to notice that the chapels in his local circuit sometimes carried the name Primitive or Wesleyan or New Connexion on the stonework near the chapel entrance. So he began to ask some of the older members what they remembered about the patterns of worship from their childhood. What he discovered helped him understand that why each chapel had subtle differences in what they expected in worship, preaching and ministry. In preparing for his work as an evangelist, he began to realize that difference contexts and histories would affect how people might be motivated towards mission and could begin to see different possibilities for different churches.

Marie, a full-time teacher, began training part-time for ordained local ministry. It was hard work trying to combine full-time work with her studies and she struggled to keep up, but after a few months, when they were given their first task, it was to be a work–life balance project and she began to look at her calling as a teacher in relation to the ideas they had been exploring about incarnation. She read a number of books and had a lot of conversations with her mentor before writing an essay on 'Being a Christian and a teacher in an assessment-driven educational system'.

These cameos are all about exploring the Christian tradition, though each has a slightly different starting point.

Pause for thought

Look at each case in turn and identify:

- What was the starting point for the study?
- What questions did each person ask about the subject in focus?
- What kinds of resources did they use to study further?

Which of these structures do you think would help you to learn most effectively?

Working at the discipline

So what is studying the Christian tradition like? Well first of all, it requires an orderly, disciplined approach. There are ways of working that need to be learned and developed. In the same way that one cannot simply pluck out a few verses of the Bible to support one's own view without accounting for other passages that present a different picture and paying close attention to the context, genre and author of the verses you choose, there are conventions that need to be understood about history and theology. It is important, for example, to know the difference between primary and secondary sources when studying Church history and use them

---

Sources

Primary sources are first-hand documents, such as the original writings of St Augustine or the sermons of John Wesley.

Secondary sources are books written by others, often later scholars, discussing original sources. E.g., books about the life and views of St Augustine or John Wesley.

In your studies you should learn to use both sources.

---

appropriately in your arguments. Likewise, ecumenical awareness is required, when looking at practical questions. For example, how should the Church practise baptism and baptismal preparation? It is not good enough simply to look at one's own experience and tradition. One needs to ask: What does my tradition and practice say, when compared with others? Do Christians in all parts of the world do the same? What different ideas are conveyed by the different practices? And what have different people said about their own Church's practice and that of others?

Second, studying the tradition requires some measure of empathy. There is an old Native American saying: 'Don't judge a man until you have worn his moccasins for a month.' In other words, you need to develop the ability to see the world through another set of eyes and appreciate the situation or circumstances of that person's life. This allows you to see why the first monks went into the desert to seek God or why the early Methodists preached in the open air. It enables you understand why Arius thought that Jesus was a 'created being' and others judged him to be wrong.

At the same time as trying to enter sympathetically into the situation, you need to hold the story at arm's length to evaluate whether you think it was the right view or action, and any conclusion you come to needs to be backed up with evidence and good argument. This is where asking questions is a good technique. Questions such as: What is the evidence for the view? Does it make sense? Are there different views? Which is strongest? This is sometimes described as a *critical approach*.

Critical is not a negative word. In the study of theology it means weighing things up, making judgements and coming to a conclusion. Being able to examine history and theology critically is a vitally important part of studying the tradition. You need to apply your mind to asking hard questions of the material you study.

Studying the tradition through:

- **Orderly investigation**
- **Empathy**
- **Asking questions**
- **Having a conversation**
- **Constructing a view**

Finally, the study of the tradition is a continual conversation or dialogue. That is, you are attempting in the first instance to grasp what happened, what was meant or what were the effects and consequences of certain actions. But you are not doing this as a disinterested person for you will bring your own thoughts, experience and views, and these will come into play as you enter into the study. This is both inevitable and desirable. This has been called using our foreknowledge, prehistory and prejudice in our study. By this means, both the tradition that you study and your own views come into a conversation. In that dialogue your understanding of both the tradition and your own views will be enlarged, challenged and perhaps changed.

For all these reasons the study of the tradition is demanding. You are seeking to engage with some of the deep and persistent questions and beliefs of the Christian faith that have been debated over centuries and continue to exercise people inside and outside of the Church. You will find you have views and feelings about many of these already and exploring them will engage you emotionally as well as intellectually. You may have to struggle hard with new ideas and how these relate to those you hold already. If you do, however, you may be able to develop your ideas further and construct new views which will strengthen your faith and help you to approach practical problems.

This leads us back to the purpose of studying the tradition. We study the tradition in order to know God better by being in a critical conversation about how the Church has responded to and expressed the love of God in the past. Knowing in this way is knowing by owning and participating in the tradition and thus allowing yourself to be an active creator as well as inheritor of the tradition.

Many conversations

We said above that in exploring the Christian tradition there is often a conversation or dialogue that goes on within you as you study. This is a dialogue between your existing views and new ones that you are encountering. But in the study of theology there are many conversations that go on. Some people envisage the study of theology as a conversation between four different partners:

Scripture: what the Bible says;

Tradition: what the Church has taught and done over its history;

Experience: our current experience both of God and the world;

Reason: what our scrutiny of the evidence and thinking shows us.

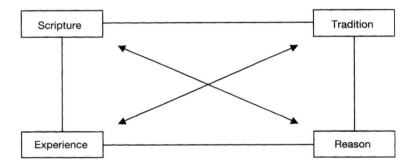

Imagine Jane from our case study above. She is concerned about baptism and what one should do when asked to baptize a baby before its death if the parents are not Christians. In her exploration she will need to look at:

- What the Bible says about baptism – and there may be different views and interpretations of the different passages.

- What the Church has taught, especially her own tradition, and why – again there may be different and even conflicting views here.

- Her experience in the hospice, with the chaplain and the parents – and she may need to look at other people's experience too.

- What her reason and thinking tells her.

While these at first sight look like a series of steps, they are more like a series of conversations between the different partners as she investigates and tries to come to a view for herself.

A living tradition

If all this sounds complicated don't be alarmed. The important thing is to see that exploring the Christian tradition is no dull exercise or hard work for nothing. Rather it is vital engagement with a living tradition.

Let me (Roger) share a story by way of illustration. When I moved to work in an area with a high burglary rate, I was told that my house would be broken into regularly (three times in the first year was the prediction). It was sobering when we were told this and it made my wife and I consider what we would least like to lose. We made a list and then cut it down and eventually the list consisted of three items. The first was my wife's engagement ring, which she could not wear at the time due to a skin problem. The second was my grandfather's pocket watch, which was not worth much in financial terms and hadn't worked from many years but had sentimental value for me. The third item was our photograph albums, which had snaps of our family and friends going back many years and several generations, to some faded brown photos where the identity of the folk on the photograph was not certain. We reckoned that should any of these items be stolen they could not be replaced. To ensure the safety of items we took two different courses of action. For the ring and the watch we arranged with the local bank to have them kept in one of their safe deposit boxes. We knew they would be as secure as possible and at any time we could go along and look at them or take one of them out for a special occasion. The photograph albums posed more problems. We wanted them to be safe, of course, but we also wanted to look at them, to show them to friends, and to add new pictures. For the photograph albums we decided that instead of putting them in a bank we would take them with us whenever we were away from the house for more than a couple of hours, and although it seems strange, we did get into the habit of carrying them with us in the car for several years.

The Christian tradition could be conceived of as the watch and the ring, needing to be kept safe in a secure place, to be checked or brought out from time to time. But I have come to think of the Christian tradition as being more like the photograph albums. These albums carry pictures of the past and with each picture there is a story that is important in the history and identity of our family (though sometimes we need an older relative to tell us the story behind a particular picture). They are reminders of what has shaped us as a family, but they are also growing in that we add new photographs on a regular basis. These new pictures are becoming part of the tradition. It is a living, growing heritage. The fact that we carried the albums with us was a reminder that the story is never separate from the present but is an integral part of an unfolding narrative. We are not predetermined by the past; we can make choices and act in new ways, but we are shaped and influenced by the history recorded in our albums; and understanding that shaping helps us make sense of and live well in the present.

It may therefore be a good way to conceptualize the Christian tradition as a rich, diverse and growing heritage of which we are part and in which we seek to live faithfully and with integrity in our own place and time. It consists of the history of the Church, its creeds, its hymns, its prayers and paintings, its formularies and confessions, its political and social actions, its arguments and its buildings, the biographies of its martyrs, leaders and individual people of faith and we as Christians are adding to the heritage daily. We have to study it to understand where we have come from, to take our place in the mission of God, to avoid reinventing the wheel and to make choices so as to live faithfully in our own day. Engaging with the tradition will require much of us but is vital if we are to be part of the unfolding story.

Going further

1. Look at your proposed programme for training. How will exploring the tradition feature in the programme?

2. Think about an issue that interests or bothers you in church life. How might you go about investigating this subject and exploring your question further?

3. It has been said that tradition is the living faith of the dead, whereas traditionalism is the dead faith of the living. What do you think this means, and do you agree with it?

Further reading

Here are some useful introductory books for exploring further the Christian tradition.

Jean Cromby, *How to Read Church History*, Volume 1, SCM Press, 1985.

Jean Cromby, *How to Read Church History*, Volume 2, SCM Press, 1989.

Trevor Hart, *Faith Thinking: The Dynamics of Christian Theology*, SPCK, 1995.

Diarmaid McCulloch, *Groundwork of Christian History*, Epworth, 1987.

Alister E. McGrath, *Theology: The Basics*, Blackwell, 2004.

Daniel L. Migliore, *Faith Seeking Understanding: An Introduction to Christian Theology*, Eerdmans, 2004.

Part Two: Knowing yourself better and being changed

5

Gifts, vocation and ministry

When I was 17 years old (writes Steven) and at the stage of
wondering what to do with my life, I was walking past the church
where I had worshipped all my life. In a single moment, in a way I
still do not understand, I had the strongest sense I have yet
known that God was calling me to Christian service and to
ordination. That call needed to be tested, first with close friends
and family and in the local church; eventually (years later) by the
diocese and the bishop and, even later, by a national selection
conference and those responsible for my training. By the time I
was ordained (nine years after the initial experience), my sense
of calling had grown and been stretched and matured and tested
through a number of life experiences and experiences in training.
I had also grown up into the calling I received many years
previously. At the time of my ordination, I assumed that I would
not have to think any more about my own calling: that it was
settled for life. In fact, I have found, the question of calling is one
which stays with us: if anything, the wrestling at different life
stages becomes deeper and more difficult as life moves on.

No two stories of a call to ministry will be the same. God will not call you in the
same way he called me. A call in early life will be different from a call in midlife. A
call in midlife is different from a call in old age. When Jesus calls Nathaniel (a
young man) at the beginning of John's Gospel, he is confident and certain, ready
to follow instantly. When he calls the Samaritan woman at the well (in midlife),
she is wondering but also cautious and hesitant, more conscious of her mistakes
in life than of her potential. When Jesus calls Nicodemus in old age, he needs
longer as a secret disciple to reflect on the costs and what this will mean.

Not many people enter initial training absolutely certain about their call. Many
begin formation for Christian ministry with great openness about what kind of
ministry they will eventually exercise. For everyone, there is a process of growing
into their calling and understanding it more. A vital element in initial training is

therefore continuing to think about your call to Christian service. In most people's experience, the need to think about vocation does not go away once an initial direction is settled but is a recurring theme throughout life. The shape of our ministry and the place where it is exercised and the mix of what we do continue to evolve. Not only that, but everyone involved in ministry will be involved at some point in helping other people to work out their calling in the life of the local church and in society. The word *vocation* means 'calling'. The word comes from the Latin *vocare* – 'to call'. Understanding vocation is a key part of formation.

There are many different resources to bring to this part of your training. This chapter aims to introduce those resources and give you an overview of them and also some sense of how they fit together.

Baptism

At the beginning of his ministry, Jesus was baptized by John. Jesus' baptism was marked by immersion in water, by words of love and affirmation from God and by Jesus being filled with the Spirit for the ministry which would follow. Following Jesus' command according to Matthew 28.19-20, the Church from its earliest days has offered baptism to those who become part of the Christian community:

> All authority in heaven and earth has been given to me. Go therefore and make disciples of all nations, baptizing them in the name of the Father and of the Son and of the Holy Spirit, and teaching them to obey everything that I have commanded you.

Check it out

Follow through these references to baptism in the book of Acts:

- Acts 2.41   The day of Pentecost
- Acts 8.9-14   The Samaritans
- Acts 8.36-38   The Ethiopian eunuch
- Acts 9.18   Saul
- Acts 10.44-48   Cornelius and his household
- Acts 16.15   Lydia and her household
- Acts 16.33-34   The Philippian jailer and his household

Like the service of Holy Communion, baptism carries a range of imagery and many layers of meaning. It is both a sign and symbol of membership of the Christian community, and also (drawing on the picture of Jesus' baptism and the gift of the Spirit) a commissioning for Christian ministry and for a life of discipleship and service. The act of going down into the water (in baptism by immersion) is a sign of complete cleansing and a new beginning, but also of one's old life dying with Christ and of rising again to live a life dedicated to God. This aspect of baptism is preserved and emphasized in the Anglican and Methodist services of confirmation (where the emphasis is again on the gift of the Spirit and the laying on of hands as a commissioning for service and adult Church membership). It is also brought out much more strongly in the new service of baptism in both our Churches where, following the baptism, the candidates are commissioned for mission and ministry. The question and answer format is similar to the commissioning in the ordination services.

Those who are baptized are called to worship and serve God.

Will you continue in the apostles' teaching and fellowship, in the breaking of bread and in the prayers?
With the help of God, I will.

Will you persevere in resisting evil and whenever you fall into sin, repent and return to the Lord?
With the help of God, I will.

Will you proclaim by word and example the good news of God in Christ?
With the help of God, I will.

Will you seek and serve Christ in all people, loving your neighbour as yourself?
With the help of God, I will.

Will you acknowledge Christ's authority over human society by prayer for the world and its leaders, by defending the weak and by seeking peace and justice?
With the help of God, I will. [1]

In the Methodist tradition this element of every Christian being called by Christ to costly discipleship and a life of service is also emphasized through the annual covenant service: a powerful invitation to a renewal of Christian commitment at the beginning of each year. The ideas in the service build on the strong biblical concept of a solemn covenant between God and his people. The covenant prayer (quoted here in its older form) emphasizes complete dedication to God's service and a determination to live out a calling to ministry.

I am no longer my own but yours.
Put me to what you will,
rank me with whom you will;
put me to doing, put me to suffering;

let me be employed for you or laid aside for you,
exalted for you or brought low for you;
let me be full, let me be empty,
let me have all things, let me have nothing;
I freely and wholeheartedly yield all things
to your pleasure and disposal.[2]

Our understanding of baptism means therefore that every disciple is committed
to wholehearted Christian service and commitment and to seeking to follow
God's call in response to God's grace. This means that the question of vocation is
not about *whether* I am called to serve God with my whole life – for every
Christian is called to this kind of service. The question of vocation is about *how I*
am called to serve God now and in the future. A vocation to recognized ministry
within the Church is not therefore to be seen in some way as 'better' or more
deeply Christian than a vocation to serve God in other ways, but simply as a
different calling. The Methodist services of ordination contain the following
paragraph at the beginning of each summary of the responsibilities of particular
ministries:

> Beloved in Christ, the Church is God's holy people, the Body of Christ, the
> dwelling place of the Holy Spirit.
>
> **All who are received into the Church by Baptism are called to**
> **proclaim the mighty acts of God in Jesus Christ our Saviour**
> **and to serve him in the Church and in the world.**
>
> God has called you into . . .[3]

All the people of God are called to service and ministry in baptism. The vocation
to recognized and authorized ministry is one calling among many in the life of the
Church.

God's gracious gifts

All ministry and service is offered back to God in a response of love and
thanksgiving to God's grace and goodness poured out to the world and in the
Church. It is important to establish this truth at the heart of our own lives and
ministry. We do not offer ourselves in ministry in order to win God's love and
favour, still less to earn our salvation or our place in heaven through our good
deeds, still less to gain power and influence and recognition for ourselves
(although all of these temptations are very real). We offer what we can
(imperfect though it is) in thankful response to what God has done in and
through Jesus Christ.

Three important passages on ministry in the New Testament demonstrate this great truth beyond any doubt. The first, Romans 12, must be understood in the context of the whole epistle. In the letter to the Romans, Paul spends eleven chapters expounding and exploring the wonderful gospel of God's grace. Through the love and grace of God and through the death and resurrection of Jesus Christ we have been justified and made right with God and given the gift of the Spirit. The righteousness we have been given is ours by grace through faith: it is not achieved by keeping laws. We do not deserve such grace and love:

> Therefore, since we are justified by faith, we have peace with God through our Lord Jesus Christ through whom we have obtained access to this grace in which we stand; and we boast in our hope of sharing the glory of God. (Romans 5.1)

It is only after eleven chapters of expounding this amazing grace that Paul turns to our response, using the language of the living sacrifice in Romans 12:

> I appeal to you therefore, brothers and sisters, by the mercies of God, to present your bodies as a living sacrifice, holy and acceptable to God, which is your spiritual worship. (Romans 12.1)

The chapter then goes on to talk about specific and diverse gifts for ministry within the same body which are offered as part of that living sacrifice. Each is to be pursued wholeheartedly and is of equal value to the body. Each is necessary for the building up of the body of Christ:

> We have gifts that differ according to the grace given to us: prophecy, in proportion to faith; ministry, in ministering; the teacher, in teaching; the exhorter, in exhortation; the giver, in generosity; the leader, in diligence; the compassionate, in cheerfulness. (Romans 12.6-8)

It is probable, though not absolutely certain, that we have here a list of 'recognized ministries': *exhortation* is a term for public teaching and preaching; the term for *ministry* is *diakonia* – already a recognized term for ministry (see Romans 16.1 and Philippians 1.1); *the giver* may refer to the person who offers help to the needy within the community (see Acts 6.1-6; the word means literally 'one who shares out'); *the compassionate* is possibly a reference to one exercising pastoral ministry or acts of mercy on behalf of the community. The verse is one of a number of early lists of ministries exercised within and on behalf of the congregation in which the early Church is feeling its way towards names and titles for authorized ministry – something which does not reach a settled form until the end of the New Testament period. What is clear for our purposes is that these ministries are all described not primarily as abilities or talents, but as gifts of

God to his Church through particular individuals who then offer those gifts wholeheartedly in the service of others.

The letter to the Ephesians follows a similar structure to the letter to the Romans with an opening chapter which expounds God's grace in all its glory. Only in chapter 4 does Paul begin to explore the implications of God's grace for the life of the Church and for Christian ministry. Once again, the letter uses the language of gift:

> The gifts he gave were that some would be apostles, some prophets, some evangelists, some pastors and teachers, to equip the saints for the work of ministry, for building up the body of Christ, until all of us come to the unity of the faith and of the knowledge of the Son of God, to maturity, to the measure of the full stature of Christ. (Ephesians 4.11-13)

Those who exercise particular and recognized ministries are God's gift to the Church. The purpose of their own ministry is to 'equip the saints' and build up the body of Christ to maturity. They themselves are given different gifts to fulfil God's calling. The list of ministries is, you will notice, different from that in Romans: only the prophets overlap. In Romans there is a greater emphasis, perhaps, on government and care of the congregation, and in Ephesians there is a greater emphasis on the wider mission of the Church (with the inclusion of apostles and evangelists).

The third of this important group of passages on ministry again uses the picture of the body and again speaks of ministry in the language of God's gracious gift. There is, once more, a difference of emphasis in the Corinthian congregation with, in this context, a stress on ministries which are connected with the direct empowering of the Spirit in the life of the Christian community. As in Ephesians, but more explicitly, there is an ordering and prioritizing of the gifts:

> Now you are members of the body of Christ and individually members of it. And God has appointed in the church first apostles, second prophets, third teachers; then deeds of power, then gifts of healing, forms of assistance, forms of leadership, various kinds of tongues. (1 Corinthians 12.27-28)

The lesson of all three passages is clear: different kinds of service are needed in the life of the Church. God gives to different individuals different gifts according to the ministry they are called to exercise. Part of learning about our own vocation is therefore about coming to understand these gifts and ministries in the life of the Church and also about understanding the gifts God is giving to us.

In developing this understanding three things are vital. The first is that we approach this task from the foundation of humility before God and before others. This is Paul's absolute starting point for thinking about ministry in Romans 12 and the theme recurs again in 1 Corinthians 12–14:

> For by the grace given to me I say to everyone among you not to think of yourself more highly than you ought to think, but to think with sober judgement, each according to the measure of faith that God has assigned. (Romans 12.3)

Humility does not mean false modesty. It does mean acknowledging that whatever gifts and abilities we have are God-given and do not thereby confer any special status or position within the body of Christ.

Second, we all need to take the time and the trouble to explore the gifts and abilities we have been given and to thank God for them. You will, no doubt, begin training with some awareness of whether you have gifts in the area of evangelism or pastoral care; whether you are effective in working with children or adults; whether you are able to lead worship and to preach God's word. It is a good thing to review regularly one's own gifts as part of a process of formation. One of the ways we grow through a formational community is by having our own gifts affirmed and reflected back to us in a supportive way by our peers and by tutors and teachers. Different descriptions and definitions of gifts can be helpful, but beware of anything where the categories are very rigid. There are ways of assessing one's gifts which seem very predetermined and do not give the flexibility to the Spirit which is there in the biblical material. Our own understanding of our gifts can be a very significant element in exploring our vocation.

However, we also need to accept that, by the grace and gifting of God, we should not think of our gifts as a package of abilities given to us once either as innate talents (when we were born) or as spiritual qualities (when we came to faith or at some later point). Nor should we think of them as only contained within the categories of these important New Testament lists (which differ according to each context). God is infinitely generous and infinitely creative. Not only is each person and ministry unique, but each person's ministry unfolds over time. We may therefore find gifts and abilities developing in midlife which we were not aware of when we were younger; or new qualities and authority given in later life for particular tasks or callings. And all gifts need to be developed: if you have a gift for preaching that does not mean you don't have to put in the hard work of engaging with the Scriptures and learning your craft. The usefulness of the qualities we have been given is likely to increase as those gifts are used. Just as our reflection on vocation needs to be continuous throughout our lives, so should be our reflection on our stewardship of own gifts and our openness to what God wants to do.

Finally, one vital element in all this theme of gifts is the mutuality of the body of Christ. God's purpose according to these passages is to distribute the necessary gifts throughout the Church, not to focus all gifts in one or two very special individuals. Often the Church has distorted this insight in the way it has focused particularly on the role of the ordained, who are seen as having every gift and insight while the rest of the body of Christ have very few. Gifts are given to the whole body to encourage mutual dependence and mutual grace and care throughout the Church. Part of the role of those called to recognized public ministries is to help others to acknowledge their own gifts and use them more fully in the service of Christ.

God's call

All Christians share in the common call to discipleship and service through baptism. All Christians are entrusted with gifts to be used in God's service. These gifts differ in different individuals. However, there is more to working out our calling than simply seeking to match our own gifts to the particular needs of the Church, like fitting pieces into a jigsaw puzzle.

The testimony of Scripture is that God's call comes to individuals also in a very personal and unique way and that God calls us not simply for our gifts but as whole people. The stories of Abraham and Moses, of Isaiah and Jeremiah, of Mary and Lydia, and many others, demonstrate that God's personal call comes to individuals to exercise a particular ministry.

Check it out

The following Bible passages are all stories of a personal call to faith and service:

- Genesis 12.1-4   Abraham
- Exodus 3.1 – 4.17   Moses
- Isaiah 6.1-13   Isaiah
- Jeremiah 1.1-10   Jeremiah
- Luke 1.26-56   Mary
- Acts 16.11-15, 40   Lydia

All of these passages and others repay careful study as you explore vocation. Each of them is different and personal: there is no absolutely standard call to ministry. In the same way no two people's story of being called will be identical. From earliest times, commentators have drawn attention to the fact that some people are called very willingly (such as Isaiah who volunteers to answer God's call) and others are called (like Jeremiah) against their own will and desires. Even those who are called willingly, as it were, have a deep sense of their own unworthiness. As you talk to different people about their sense of vocation, you may find the same distinction.

Of all the stories, the account of Moses at the burning bush is the longest and one of the earliest in the tradition. The story has probably helped to shape many of the other biblical stories of God calling people and countless other vocations to service down the centuries. The story begins through God graciously attracting Moses' attention through the bush which is burning but not consumed. A call will often intervene in our lives in unexpected ways (but ways which make sense of our earlier story). Moses' call is centred on the needs of God's people. It is a very great challenge indeed to Moses. In the narrative which follows, Moses then offers five different reasons why he should not accept the call. Each reason is answered by the Lord with a different and gracious provision for the ministry which will follow. Again the sense of wrestling with a vocation and gaining a fuller understanding of God's grace and the resources which are provided for ministry is a common experience.

This picture of God calling individuals to ministry in a variety of ways continues throughout the story of the Church in every different culture and continues still today. One of the very wonderful things about beginning training for ministry is the opportunity to share stories of God's call together and to see both similarities and differences.

The call of the community

A second major and complementary element in exploring vocation is recognizing the call of the Christian community. Again, this is a feature of call stories from earliest times. When Saul was appointed king of Israel, he had a clear and personal experience of God's call through his meeting with Samuel (you will find the story in 1 Samuel 10). However, we are also told the story of the wonderful scene where Saul is selected as king by lot in the midst of the assembly and is found hiding among the baggage. He is found and brought by force to be acclaimed as king. The story is echoed still in ordination services in the Orthodox Churches where the candidate is brought forward 'forcibly' from the midst of the community and presented to the bishop.

In the New Testament period we read of Matthias who is selected for ministry by the first group of disciples; of the seven appointed to serve the needs of the growing church in Jerusalem; and of Paul and Barnabas appointing elders in the new churches to watch over the congregations (Acts 1.15-26; 6.1-6; 14.23). Here (we assume) there must have been some element of personal vocation and a willingness to serve, but the major emphasis in each account is on the Church recognizing a need and nominating suitable people to meet that need.

In the first two of these instances in Acts, we see the beginnings of the Christian community drawing on the Old Testament tradition to create *criteria* by which to assess a vocation to a recognized ministry. The criteria for selecting Matthias are as unique as his role (seen by Acts as unique and unrepeatable). The criteria for selecting the seven are more general and can be applied to all public ministries today: 'of good standing, full of the Spirit and of wisdom'. In the later New Testament period, as patterns of ministry begin to settle into a recognizable shape, we read of more developed descriptions of these criteria for selection which reflect the responsibility of the whole Church in recognizing vocation. For the most part, these criteria are not at all about particular *gifts* – these are assumed – but about particular qualities of character seen as essential for recognized ministries. One of the best known is in 1 Timothy 3.8-13:

> Deacons likewise must be serious, not double tongued, not indulging in much wine, not greedy for money; they must hold fast to the mystery of the faith with a clear conscience. And let them first be tested; then, if they prove themselves blameless, let them serve as deacons. Women[4] likewise must be serious, not slanderers, but temperate, faithful in all things. Let deacons be married only once and let them manage their children and their households well; for those who serve well as deacons gain a good standing for themselves and great boldness in the faith that is in Christ Jesus.

These criteria for public and recognized ministries have been in continuous development and reflected upon down the centuries. They are reflected in the descriptions of ministry in services of ordination and in the questions asked of candidates. In recent years in both our Churches they have been reflected in published selection criteria for ordained and other ministries which play a part in the recognition of a person's call to a particular ministry.

The shape of the ministry

The final element in seeking to discern a call to a particular ministry is, of course, to grow and develop in your understanding of what that ministry actually entails. All ministry is in a process of rapid development and change in both the Church of England and the Methodist Church at the present time. For that reason, exploring vocation and a process of training will need to focus both on practical experience where you work alongside a pioneer minister, a deacon, an evangelist, a Reader or a parish priest, and on study and reflection as you think about and study what should be at the heart of these ministries. No one can discover everything about every ministry, so it makes good sense, where you can, to focus your exploration on the ministry to which you believe you may be called. Some ideas for further reading are given below.

The cost of exploring vocation

Following Jesus is rarely easy. There is certainly a cost in seeking to discover and discern God's call. The process can be demanding in terms of time and energy. There is often a financial cost for those called to full-time ministry. A calling to ministry in later life means that time is taken from a job or profession you may love or else giving sacrificially in retirement. The ministry to which you are called may be extremely fulfilling, yet there may also be aspects which are difficult and demanding. All of these costs may need to be carried to some degree by your family and closest friends. As Jesus' parables indicate, assessing this cost is part of what it means to think through your vocation.

Yet there are other costs as well, which for most people are even more difficult to bear. There is undoubtedly a sense of risk in offering yourself for a recognized ministry. You may believe that God is calling you to a particular role. You may believe that you have the necessary gifts, skills and capacity. However, that calling needs to be weighed and tested by the Church through interviews and selection processes which can themselves be demanding. If the outcome of those selection processes is to affirm your own sense of calling then this will, of course, mean that sense of call is strengthened. However, if the outcome is not to affirm your sense of call but to encourage you to think in terms of a different form of Christian service, this can be very difficult. You will need the support of others who have shared the journey with you and sometimes the advice of vocational advisers to help you adjust to and find this different calling and to see it worked out in practice.

Putting it all together

All who are received into the Church by baptism are called to proclaim the mighty acts of God in Jesus Christ our Saviour and to serve him in the Church and in the world.[5]

There are many different ways of proclaiming the mighty acts of God and serving God in the Church and in the world. Exploring your vocation in its broadest sense is the task of every Christian. How are you called to serve God in your working life and in volunteer ministry? Are you, for the present, fully committed to being a carer or homemaker on behalf of others? Do you see your vocation and ministry primarily fulfilled in and through your work (if you are called to be a teacher, a youth leader or a crossing patrol warden)? Do you see your past or present work as a way of supporting your family financially so that you have some time to give in addition to recognized ministry? This is the approach followed by the apostle Paul who was self-supporting through his craft of tent-making. Do you see yourself as called to some kind of recognized and paid ministry in the life of the Churches or of a Christian organization? How should any of these particular callings be shaped and reshaped and revisited with the passage of time as circumstances change and as you yourself grow and change through life?

The way in which you answer these questions will depend in part on laying a sure foundation in your understanding of vocation as rooted in baptism and each person's call to serve and to offer their lives to God. It will depend in part on your own and other people's discernment about the gifts you are able to bring to ministry and service in the world and in the Church. This means getting to know yourself and taking time to explore the different ways in which God may have gifted you. It will depend in part on your own particular sense of God's call to service as that emerges through the years. For some people such a vocation is clear in a moment and (sometimes) quite dramatic. For others it emerges little by little with growing clarity over many years. To understand such a calling better needs time and prayer and helpful guidance on the journey. It also means growing in your understanding of the particular ministry you are called to exercise. Finally, if you are called to a life of service outside the Church then this needs no formal recognition by the Christian community (although the support of that community is vital). However, if you are called to a recognized Christian ministry in or on behalf of the Church then this call needs also to be subject to the discernment of that community. If your ministry will be in the local church (to be a Sunday School teacher or house group leader) then the discernment will normally be exercised mainly by the local church, often in informal ways. If your ministry be in the circuit, diocese or Connexion then that discernment will be exercised in that wider context.

A personal story

As I (Steven) have indicated throughout this chapter, a vocation is not something that is settled at a particular period in life and then goes away, but something which unfolds in different and often very challenging ways as life itself unfolds. At a particular moment in my own ministry I had been ordained as a curate for some years but needed to make a decision about when and whether to move on to a different post and was faced with a number of different options (at least in theory!). I found myself becoming very anxious about which path I should pursue. All kinds of different scenarios and questions become confused in my mind. At the time, I had a good relationship with an excellent spiritual director. In many ways, building a relationship with him was worth the investment of three years of meeting for a moment of this kind. I took the question to him. On the basis of our previous conversations he was able to recommend that I simply make the prayer in Isaiah 6 my own prayer for the next stage of ministry: 'Lord, here I am. Send me!'

It sounds easy enough to do. As soon as I began to pray the words, I realized that for me at that time things were not quite so simple. I wanted to be able to pray the prayer with integrity and openness, but actually it became clear that I wanted God to answer it only in a very limited number of ways (each of which, of course, satisfied my own sense of ambition or self-importance). There followed something of a period of struggle and other conversations and journaling until by God's grace I did reach the point where it was possible to pray the prayer and mean it: 'Lord, here I am. Send me!' At that point (and at exactly that point on this occasion) the way ahead became absolutely and unmistakably crystal clear.

Going further

1.   Read through the baptism service and an ordination service. What are the similarities and the differences?

2.   What do you think are the main areas where you are gifted? Make a short list and ask the opinion of two or three other people who know you well.

3.   What is the story of you following your sense of God's call to the present moment? Either tell it to someone else or write it down in your journal.

Further reading

Steven Croft, *Ministry in Three Dimensions: Ordination and Leadership in the Local Church*, Darton, Longman & Todd, 1999.

Francis Dewar, *Called or Collared*, SPCK, 1991.

Philip Luscombe and Esther Shreeve (eds), *What is a Minister?*, Epworth Press, 2002.

6

Understanding formation

Some people entering preparation for ministry are surprised by the use of the word *formation*. It is not one that they have associated with learning before and it can also have worrying undertones. In theological institutions, where the word formation is often used, one sometimes hears new students asking, 'What is formation? When is it going to start? How will it happen? Who is going to do it to us? Will it hurt?'

The basic fear behind the nervousness expressed in some of those questions is to do with the idea that someone else will be doing things to you, someone else has control, someone else knows what the outcome is meant to be and is planning the process so that this happens to you. In other words, there is a fear that you are an object to be shaped and moulded and you might not have any power over what happens. When students begin a course, there is sometimes an expectation that the aim is to turn out people who are all alike; the course or college may be known as a Vicar Factory.

There is some truth here mixed in with some groundless fear. Formation does imply one who forms, but according to the Bible it is God, in a loving relationship, who makes and shapes us. It is God in Christ and through the Spirit who creates, forms and transforms us. Human beings and communities may be the agents of God, but the primary agent is God, who is forming us according to God's loving purpose. In the process God gives and respects human freedom and thus invites us to cooperate in this formation rather than imposing upon or overriding our will. Individuals are free to choose to participate in the forming process.

Perhaps equally important is that the outcome of this divine formation is not a predetermined, fixed shape. It is not a mould that produces the same figure each time it is used. Rather this forming by God, which is accomplished through relationship, enables growth and development that is individual and unique to each person. Parents who produce two or more children sometimes marvel at how vastly different their children are from one another. This is despite the fact that these offspring are from the same two parents, have grown up in the same household with the same rules, patterns and values and being subject to the same discipline and experiences. Others looking at these children will see a strong family resemblance and shared characteristics alongside the individuality of each member of the family. Christian formation is like this. It is a forming by relationship which reflects both the character of the one who forms, and the uniqueness, individuality and choices of those who are formed.

Check it out

Read Psalm 139.

In what ways does the writer see God shaping him or her? Where in the Psalm is the willingness to cooperate expressed?

Now look at the following verses. What do they say about formation?

- **Romans 8.29**
- **Galatians 4.19**
- **Colossians 3.9-10**
- **Ephesians 4.22-25**
- **Romans 12.2**

Clearly then, formation does not just apply to preparation for ministry. It is going on in all our lives and especially in our Christian discipleship as we seek to discern and respond to God. It is, however, a useful word for understanding what is happening to us in the process of preparation for ministry.

Which word?

There are other terms which can be and are used to describe preparation for ministry. *Training* is sometimes used. It is useful word and captures some of what is going on in the process. It suggests the development of practical skills, such as preaching, pastoral care, running a kids' holiday club or conducting a funeral. People learn how to do these things through a combination of observation, reflection, reading and thinking about key principles, supervised participation, personal practice and feedback. The outcome is that they become competent and can be trusted to carry out duties professionally and proficiently. The language of 'training' can be used, however, in a rather functional way that focuses on the acquisition of skills to the detriment of a broader development of character. In the end, it is not enough to be able to carry out the functions competently. In Christian ministry we are called also to embody the values of Christ in what we do. As St Paul says, 'If I speak to you in the tongues of mortals and of angels, but do not have love, I am a noisy gong or a clanging cymbal' (1 Corinthians 13.1). Training is not sufficient on its own.

The language of *education*, on the other hand, is a rich and ancient one, with its root meaning of *educare* being to draw out. Thus education can be the drawing out of the human person and the development of the full potential of both individuals and communities through the learning process. However, the notion of education is unhelpful to many people in thinking about learning in the life of the Church because it is so strongly associated with formal learning within the context of schooling. In the community of the Church we are concerned with a whole variety of ways and contexts of learning, and it may be helpful to employ a different kind of language which will draw attention to these.

In recent years the words training, education and formation have been held together as indicating different aspects of the process, but many have come to prefer the word formation as best suited to understanding the experience of preparation for ministry – partly because it can incorporate the other two terms, but mainly because it resonates with the biblical picture of God and how God works with human beings.

Biblical roots

In the Old Testament it is God who forms the earth (Psalm 90), God who forms human beings (Genesis 2.7) and every bird and animal (Genesis 2.19), God who forms the nation and his people (Isaiah 43.1,7,21), God who forms individuals in the womb with tender love (Jeremiah 1.5; Psalm 139.16) and God who forms the individual parts of the body and the human spirit (Psalm 94.9; Zechariah 12.1). There are some references to human beings forming things, but most references are to God's activity of forming. When it comes to the forming of individuals, peoples or nations the (Hebrew and corresponding Greek) word is never used of human activity.

Many different images of this work of formation are offered. God is imaged as the original speaker or singer who fashions by word and by breath (Genesis 1; Sirach 24.3). God is pictured as a creative artist who fashions the earth as a potter fashions the clay (Isaiah 29.16; Jeremiah 18.6; Romans 9.20-24); as a weaver who knits together and intricately weaves the human person within the womb (Psalm 139.13-15); or as a mother who bears and brings forth from her own body a new creation (Deuteronomy 32.18).

In the New Testament, this emphasis on the creating and forming work of God is refocused in Christ. Here there is a recurring theme of being conformed and transformed into the image of Christ, of Christ being formed in the believer and in the community of the Church (Romans 8.29; Galatians 4.19; 1 Corinthians 15.49; 2 Corinthians 3.18; Colossians 3.9-10; Ephesians 4.23; Romans 12.2; Philippians 3.9-21; Colossians 1.27-28). The goal of learning and growth in faith is not only that we may come to know about Christ, nor even that we might know Christ, but that, in some extraordinary way, Christ may become formed in us;

even, we might dare to say, that we might *become* Christ. This is our destiny: divinization, as the Eastern Orthodox Church would call it, or sanctification, in Wesleyan terms – to become Christ-like.

The same conviction, that it is God who is forming us to be Christ-like, remains behind these texts. Paul does suggest, however, that others can share in this forming work of God in Christ. He declares that he, himself, is in travail (painful childbirth) until Christ is formed in his Galatian readers (Galatians 4.19). The epistle to the Ephesians likewise suggests that believers share in the forming of one another. As we grow up into Christ (Ephesians 4.15), we grow as a body in which as every part is working properly the body builds itself up in love (Ephesians 4.16). That means that as well as seeking to cooperate with God, we are called also to work with another in the process of formation.

Pause for thought

Make a short list of the people and groups that have helped you in the forming of your life and faith to date. In what ways did each influence or affect you?

Formation for God[1]

How does God form us? There seem to be patterns or principles that regularly recur.

We are formed in and through our humanity

It is not that God wants us to stop being human beings or in some ways overcome our humanness in order to share in the divine nature. Rather it is, paradoxically, that by becoming refocused on God we become more our human selves. As Irenaeus, one of the early Church leaders, put it, '*The glory of God is a human being fully alive.*' Formation, then, will take place not outside our human everyday experience but in and through it. It will be in the daily contact with others that we are formed and our whole person will be involved and affected. It will be in particular and concrete incidents, events and encounters that we are challenged or changed.

We are formed by a journey through life and death

Our formation to be like Christ and to be truly ourselves takes a lifetime. It is a lifelong journey. Some of the journey is exciting and joy-filled, but equally some of it a hard, painful struggle. Easter gives us a picture of new life coming after and through death. When Jesus says 'Unless a grain of wheat falls into the earth and dies, it remains just a single grain; but if it dies, it bears much fruit' (John 12.24), he is referring to his own life but also pointing to the nature of Christian pilgrimage and the character of Christian forming. Letting go of the old must occur in order that the new may be born; the deconstruction of old patterns and forms of thinking, feeling and acting, both in ourselves and in the Church, needs to happen so that God can fashion a new shape. We should expect throughout life that these mini experiences of death and new life are an important part of the formation process.

We are formed in and for community

We are sometimes tempted to think of formation as simply the formation of an individual person, but a strong theme of the New Testament is the formation of Christ in the body of believers. We are a body in which each part needs the other parts. As the passage from Ephesians reminds us, it is when all the parts are working together that growth occurs. In other words, Christ is formed in the Church as we work with and for each other. The fact that church communities and training courses are often made up of people who are different from each other is a strength in this process. Engaging with folk who are 'not like us', as we seek to live as God's people, enables formation and change.

We are formed in and for the transformation of the world

Finally we need to keep God's perspective and purpose in mind when we consider formation. God's intention is not simply to form the Church or individuals. Ultimately God's relationship is with the world. As John 3.16 reminds us, 'God so *loved the world* that he gave his only son'; and, as Paul writes, 'the creation itself will be set free' by God's liberating and transforming love (Romans 8.21). Thus our formation will be in part through our engagement with issues of local, national and international life. God forms us as we get involved in the issues of our workplace or local community, as we seek justice for asylum seekers or struggle with how to care for the planet. The fact that there are no easy answers to some of these problems means that we must be more open to God's purpose.

Deconstruction and formation

For the formation to happen well in training, most people find there are some elements of untangling and unpicking of ideas or habits. The ground needs to be cleared, often, before something new can be created. For this reason, a community of people 'in formation' is almost always a demanding community to be part of for any length of time. When we spend time together forming close relationships, we bring with us the normal difficulties and challenges of life as well as the particular issues with which we wrestle from day to day.

Sometimes, courses of study or tutorial relationships are deliberately constructed to include this element of deconstruction before rebuilding can begin (thankfully more in the past than in the present). In our own view, deliberately introducing these elements into the formational process is unhelpful and confuses the role and responsibilities of the tutorial staff (to build people up not tear them down).

The Rule of Benedict contains wise advice for all communities of formation. In particular, Benedict establishes at the beginning of his Rule the vital principle of gentleness in discipleship and disciple-making:

> We have, therefore, to establish a school of the Lord's service. In instituting it we hope to establish nothing harsh or oppressive.[2]

The words translated 'harsh' and 'oppressive' here mean literally 'nothing heavy or sharp'. Those guiding communities of formation, according to Benedict, have the responsibility to do all they can to remove deliberate sharpness and heaviness. Even more alien to the spirit of Benedict is deliberately to aim, as it were, to deconstruct peoples' lives or faith intentionally as part of formation. When all that is sharp and heavy is removed, you will normally find that there is difficulty enough in living together, in the normal trials, tribulations and challenges life brings and in the ideas each person brings to provide grit for the oyster.

Formation for ministry

In preparation for ministry we can expect our formation to continue through the same patterns that God uses to form us throughout our lives. Our everyday encounters will still be a place where we are formed, we will continue to have mini experiences of death and new life, engagement with the issues of the world will still be required of us and we will go on delighting and struggling in community, though the community experience may now involve those with whom we study. The danger is to think that formation will somehow be apart from all of this, that formation will happen only in the special activities and studies of the programme. If we think that, however, we may begin to think of God's activity as confined only to the religious sphere or to the structure and content of our course and that would suggest a smaller, more limited God. It might also lead to us missing some of the things God is saying or doing because we are looking in the wrong place. The truth is that the new programme will be woven into the broader, ongoing pattern of God's forming work.

There is, on the other hand, a new *focus* for our formation in preparation for ministry. By definition training for the Church's ministry is getting ready for a public role where in some form you will represent the Church to others. To do this you need to develop as a person in a role. Whatever skills and knowledge you need to take up this role, you will also need to have formed a Christian character appropriate for responsibilities. A doctor who has learned excellent surgical skills and a compendium of medical knowledge would be still be unhelpful to people if she constantly undermined people's confidence in the local health service by telling them horror stories about failed operations or gossiping details told in the confidence of the consultation room. The character of a doctor needs to form so that he has confidence in his work and his calling and people can have confidence in him. Likewise, a minister needs to develop a disposition and character suitable for representing the Church in the public domain.

What this means in preparation is the formation of a whole person for the work and thus there will be elements and processes in the programme designed to help the development of character. The activities may cluster around three basic principles.

Extending your experience

As a trainee preacher, pastoral worker, evangelist or priest, you will come to your course with experience of at least one church community. You may have experience of more than one church, but the programme will almost certainly extend this so you have experiences of new church communities, possibly in very different settings. If you know what an Anglican village parish is like, you may be given experience of a large suburban church or inner city mission. If you have worshipped in a town church all your life you may train to be a local preacher by conducting services in a series of country chapels. If you have visited housebound people regularly you may have a placement in a children's hospital. Clearly doing this will give you more experience of different contexts and may extend your range of skills. It will also give you a new perspective on your local or sending church community. But it has a further purpose, which is to do with learning what it means to be a minister and to represent the Church in all these settings. Having a sense of the diversity and richness of the Church strengthens your sense of God's work. It also helps you to discern the role of the minister in public settings, act in ways that are appropriate, and integrate these actions and attitudes into your character.

Learning to inhabit a public role

In our training college we had a policy that those training to be Methodist presbyters could wear clerical collars for hospital visits and other similar occasions when on placement. We encouraged them to do this and then to reflect on how people reacted to them. One person said it appeared to 'open doors' with some people and 'close them' with others. Another student, who was often outspoken about some of the failings of the Church, said she struggled with the idea of putting on the clerical shirt because she realized that once she put it on and people saw her they would assume that she was in part responsible for some of those failings that she complained about. By trying on the clothes, both students learned something about what it means to represent the Church and be identified publicly with its life and mission. You may or may not have exactly this experience in your preparation for ministry, but there are a number of activities that will allow you to begin to inhabit the role of a minister. If you are training for ordination (or think that is a possibility), try the radical experiment of folding up a piece of white card and pushing it into your collar – then look in a mirror or talk to a friend. See what a difference it makes at first.

Placing things in a bigger context

Alongside these stretching experiences you will also be encountering many ways of thinking about your calling through your academic studies. You will meet different models of ministry, different views of mission, different interpretations of biblical passages and different approaches to worship and theology. All this is part of locating yourself in relation to the big picture of the Church and its calling. This too can be formational, in that it forms us to see and take our place in the much bigger work that God has been doing in a multitude of ways over thousands of years and in a multitude of cultures.

Elements that may quicken the process

Formation is a large and complex process and many things feed into it. There are a few key elements, however, in the course you will be part of.

Peer groups

People who starting training with you and make the same journey as you may well become not only fellow students but also a group with whom you share your developing ideas, struggles, failures and successes and thus they become (often lifelong) friends. In many ways you may trust these people more than staff of institutions especially in the early stages. You may trust them with some of your most personal confidences and find that you pray for them and they for you regularly. You may also discuss, debate and disagree with them and clash with them over important issues. It is impossible to do all this and not be shaped by the experience. Much of the formational energy in preparing for ministry is found among peers.

Tutorial and mentor relationships

Tutors are appointed in part to support people as they negotiate their preparation and manage change. Regular meetings can be where much of the personal reflection and integration takes place. It is in these conversations that the disparate elements of people's training – their study, their placement work, their personal questions and issues – can be brought together. There may not be a formal tutor on your programme, but there may be a mentor, an experienced minister with whom you can have the same relationship. Here too it may be you can tackle everything from practical advice to exploring personal crises. No one can guarantee that two people will get on or develop trust. The chemistry may simply be wrong. But where these relationships develop they often have a profound influence on us and help in our formation. I (Roger) can still remember life-changing conversations with my college tutor from 30 years ago.

Assessment

Essays, examinations, formal interviews or presentations are often seen as unpleasant hurdles that have to be jumped at some stage in our training and as such their formational influence is underestimated. The reality is that preparing and writing assignments will require much of our thinking energy and thus will form both the ideas we own and the ways we think about issues. The same is true about a seminar we might lead or sermon we preach that others hear and assess. Later in the book we will explore assessment in more detail. For now we should realize this factor will also be formative for us.

Your own gifts and passions

In all this discussion about formation it is important to remember what we said at the beginning, that God is working not to make us all identical – like the people in the old song who are 'made out of ticky-tacky and all look the same' – but to form unique people for God's purposes. While we may be preparing to be in public ministry and thus need to form some of the dispositions and character that will serve the Church, we also have particular gifts and experiences that God will continue to strengthen and develop. What is more, we will have our own passions, things we desire and have energy for, and it is important to allow these to grow too.

A recent report on church ministry suggested that in the midst of all the things a presbyter or priest may have to do – administration, preaching, visiting, leading nurture groups, relating to the local community, conducting funerals, baptisms, weddings and the thousand and one things that are expected – each minister should devote at least 25 per cent of his or her time to working at the things for which they have real passion and enthusiasm. It was suggested that doing this would in itself be a stimulus to all the other work and allow the person to be constantly encouraged and energized. The same could be said of the work of a deacon, a Reader or an evangelist: we need to be engaging in something which energizes us for at least part of our ministry.

If this is true in ministry, it is also true in preparation for ministry. Pursue your own passions and calling, not as an alternative to the formational pattern of the programme but alongside it and with it, so that God can form both the person and the ministry God desires.

How does formation feel?

At the end of initial training for ministry people often reflect on what the journey has been like. When they do they regularly speak in terms like these: 'It was like God opening me up to grow into a bigger person'; 'I feel like I have the same clothes that I packed in the suitcase at the beginning but I have taken them all out and repacked them in a different way'; 'Now I feel I am living in a bigger picture.' Perhaps most significantly of all, people begin to use the language of becoming and say things like, 'I am unsure exactly what God is making of me, but I feel as if I am growing up into the person he wants me to be.' These phrases point towards a deep sense people have that God has been forming them for ministry and will not stop when the course finishes.

Going further

1. Identify for yourself what has been the most formative experience of your life so far.

2. Try to imagine what would be the features of a more fully formed you in relation to the calling you are pursuing. What would be characteristics of that formed person? How might you begin to move towards the vision?

3. Talk to someone who has finished the course you are about to follow. Ask them how they changed over the time and what helped them grow.

Further reading

Rosalind Brown and Christopher Cocksworth, *Being a Priest Today: Exploring Priestly Identity*, Cowley, 2004.

Philip Luscombe and Esther Shreeve (eds), *What is a Minister?*, Epworth Press, 2002.

Henri Nouwen, *The Wounded Healer: Ministry in Contemporary Society*, Darton, Longman & Todd, 1994.

Michael Ramsey, *The Christian Priest Today*, SPCK, 1985.

7

Balancing life

Living and learning well is often about finding the right balance in our lives. The different parts of our life may bring blessings, but they also make demands on our time and our energy. When our life is going well and feels manageable, these different demands are in balance. However, there are times for all of us when these demands become too great and life feels seriously out of balance and too demanding. We may cope with this well in the short term. However, if it continues in the long term we may be seriously overstretched in a number of different directions: our health, our key relationships, our motivation and the quality of our work may all begin to suffer. A gap appears between our outer life and the inner reality.

Training alongside employment

Entering a process of training for recognized ministry is one of those periods in life when this balance will be challenged and changed in a number of different ways. If you are training for ministry alongside your employment and other commitments (the experience of most people), then the challenge will be to find space and time in your life for course contact time (midweek evenings or Saturday mornings or residential weekends); energy and time for new relationships with fellow students and staff; new contexts for ministry and, of course, the reading and assessed work which forms part of any programme of study. However enjoyable and stimulating these different, new things are, finding appropriate space for them with your present commitments may be hard. Some people begin this form of training at a point when there are other life changes taking place (such as children leaving home or taking early retirement). If that is the case, the changes brought by training are simply part of a wider change taking place in life. For others, life continues much as usual with a series of *additional* calls on their time. For all, hopefully, there will be some space created by stepping back from other ministerial responsibilities and commitments at least for a time. Finding a new balance therefore requires for everyone a certain amount of thinking, reflection and support in the early part of your period of training.

'Full-time' training

Other people, of course, have the very different experience of being able to give their whole time to the process of training and formation for a period of one, two or three years. This process generates very different opportunities, questions and challenges. Moving to a new area and what is probably a completely different way of life and community presents its own good things and also challenges for those in training and often for their families. For many people the new beginning is positive and stretching with opportunities for new friendships and community as well as time to study without also having to support yourself through paid work. However, it can be hard to leave behind the rhythms and routines of a job you have enjoyed for many years and which has given you a sense of fulfilment, of position and status and a shape to the week and to the year (and, perhaps, also a good income). It can be hard beginning life in a new community where life is shaped around a daily rhythm of prayer, meals together and academic work (particularly if this is an area where you don't feel too confident at first). All kinds of things can be temporarily thrown out of balance: your sense of who you are, your confidence in your own skills, your ability to shape life and to manage your own time. As we shall see in the next chapter, there are many opportunities for personal change and growth in all of these times of transition. Nevertheless part of the challenge of the early period of training is to find a new and fruitful equilibrium: a new life balance as a basis for your preparation and work.

Lessons for ministerial life

There is a temptation for everyone involved in training to see these lessons of life balance to be limited just to the particular period of time in training before you begin ministry. This is a great mistake. All of these issues of life balance have a huge relevance to the ongoing work of ministry. The lessons, principles and skills you learn about balance during your years of training have the potential to be enormously helpful to your future ministry. In a similar way, the bad habits or poor theology you have now (or may develop during training) have the potential to damage your future ministry.

An equally common temptation is to regard the period of training as in some way an especially demanding time of life when other relationships and needs are, as it were, put on hold for a two- or three-year period and you live with life being out of balance for a period. Again this is a dangerous view for a number of reasons. In the first place, most people find that ministry after initial training is at least as demanding as the period of training itself. The second is that important life relationships and personal needs (for rest, recreation and friendship) cannot simply be put on hold: there are consequences in those life choices which may affect families and life patterns for many years.

The person who is training alongside their existing life and work will have the experience of having to balance a number of different and competing demands: to do their daily work well; to have time for family and close friends and for themselves; and to have time and space to attend classes, write the essays and take part in the weekends away. The same person is preparing for a ministry in which he or she will need to balance and prioritize a number of different and competing demands of time and energy including (of course) personal time and time for family and close friends. If you exercise your ordained ministry alongside or through your workplace, the challenges will be very similar to those in training. Sermon and service preparation will replace the writing of essays; ministry responsibilities will replace attending classes. If you are preparing for stipendiary ministry, then you will still find yourself balancing and prioritizing (for example) the demands of one church in the circuit against the demands of another; fitting in the building project alongside being a school governor; finding time for sermon preparation in a week when you are taking several funerals.

The person who leaves work and trains in a college setting is learning hugely important lessons about transition and change and entering a new community: skills which are vital to exercising full-time ministry over a number of years. Learning how to live within, shape and sometimes resist in healthy ways the expectations of a Christian community is a vital preparation for church leadership. Coping with the demands of essays and academic work alongside placements, community life, family and shaping a new life in a new place, all build skills for living and shaping life and work which are important for the future. Some of the most valuable potential for learning and for change in every experience of training is in exactly these areas of life balance. You may be able to think without too much difficulty of people whose ministry is far less effective than it might be because of chronic overwork, of too much activity, of poor time management, of continually being stressed, ill and tired, of reactive patterns of ministry. You may even be able to think of ways in which your own life and ministry have been affected by all of these things. See your period in training as an opportunity to grow new and better life skills in these areas.

Pause for thought

How well has your life been balanced over the last few years?

What have been the good and the difficult elements in the mix?

How do you think beginning training will affect your equilibrium?

A culture of busyness and activity

It is vital to recognize that our culture shapes us in particular ways. One of the dominant features of most of life in Britain in the early twenty-first century is that of overwork and over-busyness in many different areas of life and in many people's experience. For a variety of complex reasons, the society we live in has lost a common sense of how to live wisely and within its limits of time, energy and money. Many people are overextended in all of these areas – some just in one or two. This is especially the case in midlife when we work more hours than our parents or grandparents. The factors behind this cultural climate are varied: they include the massive range of opportunities and choices open to us; rising expectations in every area of life; consumer choice; a more fluid society which leads to high expectations in the workplace; the rise of the information age; the culture of inspection and review which permeates every area of life; and the importance of the global market in many areas of work.

The symptoms of this over-busy, overstretched and disorganized life are easy to detect all around us. One recent survey estimated that most senior professionals now experience the phenomena of burnout at least once during their working life and often twice. Burnout is the state where being overextended results in a minor or major emotional breakdown: we simply cannot continue to function at the same pace and need time out. There is a huge cost in terms of personal life, work, marriage relationships (whether actual breakdown or loss of intimacy), friendships, parenting and in other ways.

Twenty years ago, Gordon MacDonald published one of the modern classics for Christian ministers, *Ordering your Private World*. It is still well worth reading (or rereading) particularly in times of great change. He draws up the following accurate and uncomfortable list of symptoms of a disorganized life:

- My desk takes on a cluttered appearance.

- The condition of my car deteriorates.

- I become aware of a diminution in my self-esteem.

- There are a series of forgotten appointments, telephone messages to which I have failed to respond and deadlines which I have begun to miss.

- I tend to invest my energies in unproductive tasks.

- I feel badly about my work.

- I rarely enjoy intimacy with God.

- The quality of my personal relationships declines.

- When I am disorganized I just don't like myself, my job or much else.[1]

As Christians, we cannot help being shaped to some extent by the culture in which we find ourselves. It is the air we breathe. But we will also need to recognize that there are some important ways in which as Christian ministers we will need to be counter-cultural and provide an alternative model. In this respect, unless we attempt to resist the broad direction of our culture, we may be swept along with it. As Paul writes in Romans 12.2:

> Do not be conformed to this world, but be transformed by the renewing of your minds, so that you may discern what is the will of God – what is good and acceptable and perfect.

Stress and identity

There have been a range of studies and books on clergy stress in recent years. All of them identify overactivity and overwork as real dangers. Most of them apply in different ways to those exercising lay as well as ordained ministry. Some of the books attempt to tackle the problem by dealing with what is on the surface – for example by teaching better time management skills. Generally speaking, these books are not very convincing overall (although some of the advice can be useful). If I am overextended and learn better time management skills, the outcome will probably be that I use those skills to fit in even more work! The really good and worthwhile studies of ministerial stress attempt to look beneath the surface and seek to identify some of the underlying causes of why lay and ordained ministers succumb to the temptation to work too hard (even, apparently, more than others in a culture of over-busyness). One of the consequences of work being out of balance over time is, of course, that it is done much less effectively.

One of the best studies is by Andrew Irvine, a Canadian psychologist and minister and is a study conducted over many years of ministers in the Church of Scotland. Irvine traces the causes of clergy stress to two principal root causes: identity and isolation. We will look at his material on isolation in Chapter 8. Irvine found in his interviews with ministers that the question of identity is a very serious contributor to stress and to over-busyness. This question in turn arises from the very profound change which the Church as a whole is experiencing in relation to the society in which we are set.

Again, we explore that change in more detail in Chapter 11. At its heart, however, the problem is simply stated. The role of the Church in relation to society is in a process of change: the minister's role is changing both in relation to society as a whole (in terms of status, perceptions, opportunities and work) and in relation to the Church. Navigating this change is a complex and demanding process for all Christian ministers. Sometimes, ministers seek to come to terms with these changes by trying to fulfil a vast and impossible range of expectations from their community, from society and from themselves, trying on a range of different identities. This in turn can commonly lead to over-busyness and overactivity.

Irvine is clear that in such a time it is absolutely vital for the whole Church to rethink the ministerial calling and sense of identity not simply by reacting to what is happening in Church and society now, but by going back to our sense of what should shape Christian ministry in Scripture and in the Christian tradition. We need to use our tradition to forge a new understanding of what it means to serve God's people in a recognized ministry in this particular time and place. If Irvine is right, more time needs to be given now than a generation ago to thinking through this sense of ministerial identity both for those who are already in ministry and for those in training.

Another very helpful and similar picture of what is happening to ministers is offered by Alan Roxburgh. Roxburgh has coined the phrase 'double-loop liminality' to describe the demanding experience of Christian ministers in today's rapidly changing society. *Liminal* means being at the edge or on the threshold. The first liminality ministers experience is that the whole Church has moved in the last two generations from being near the centre of our society to being at the edge. However, at the same time, society itself is changing profoundly in such a way that it no longer has a clear and stable centre in any case but is continually evolving in new ways. The instinct of the Churches is to try and regain the centre ground again – but just as we arrive at where we think it is, the centre has moved! Roxburgh writes of the uncertain identities of those in ministry:

> [T]he temptation is to find a symbolic reintegration of pastoral identity
> and a role fit to deal with the loss of symbolic identity. But many of these
> roles are borrowed from symbols that have place and prominence in the
> wider culture. What this suggests is that the level of role confusion for the
> pastor in liminality is extremely high. For example, the pastor is clinician
> (therapeutic metaphor), chaplain (institutional metaphor), coach (sports
> metaphor), entrepreneur, marketer and strategist (business metaphors).
> Beside the Bible, pastors must read John Bradshaw, know the Twelve Step
> process, discuss co-dependence, memorize the business strategies of
> Attila the Hun and understand the new non-lateral leadership paradigm
> of Peter Senge.[2]

Like Irvine, Roxburgh argues that the way to rediscover identity and purpose (and therefore a new equilibrium) is to think deeply once again about Scripture and the tradition to rediscover what it means to exercise pastoral ministry in a changing society.

In finding balance in ministry or in preparation for ministry we need to recognize the habits and ideas we bring with us from the general culture we inhabit and the particular pressures upon ministerial life. If we are honest, our search for balance will take us much deeper than learning how to use our time well to challenge some of our deeply held (if unconscious) beliefs about life, work and ministry.

Personal responsibility

As we have seen, Paul's speech to the elders of Ephesus is one of the great New Testament passages which have shaped the Churches' understanding of ministry down the centuries. At the heart of his address, Paul delivers the following charge:

> Keep watch over yourselves and over all the flock, of which the Holy Spirit has made you overseers. (Acts 20.28)

The Church down the centuries has drawn from this and other biblical passages the concept that Christian ministers must watch over and take responsibility for their own lives as part of their wider responsibility. This duty is of first importance because without it a person cannot exercise proper care of others. The concept echoes down the years in many different Christian traditions. Acts 20.28 is the key text and gives shape to some of the greatest discourses on ministry: the Pastoral Rule of Gregory the Great from the sixth century; *The Reformed Pastor* by Richard Baxter, written in 1655, and others.

The concept is there also – not surprisingly – in modern writing outside the Churches on personal development and growth. Stephen Covey's now classic text, *The Seven Habits of Highly Effective People* is about building effectiveness through building character. It is a book written particularly for those who overextend themselves: who may achieve great things in the public sphere but whose inner world is not in order. At the heart and the very beginning of the seven habits is taking responsibility for one's own growth and development and being proactive.

It is a common thing in both preparation for ministry and the exercise of ministry to find people blaming their own busyness, overextension or lack of balance on other people or other circumstances. It is all the fault of the college or course (which is unreasonable in its demands); the PCC (which sets too high expectations); of the bishop (who never rings to ask how I am); or the Church generally (which has lost direction). There is certainly a place for recognizing weaknesses in institutions and in other people. However, there is a fine line between recognizing those weaknesses on the one hand and, on the other, devolving responsibility for my own life, growth and development onto these situations. We are called to serve in an imperfect Church in an imperfect world. The same is true of Christian ministers in every generation and every place. As far as we can, therefore, we must take responsibility for the inward and outward ordering of our own lives and for finding balance within the different circumstances we are called to face.

Resources from the tradition

There are many different resources from the Christian tradition – sources other Christians have used down the years as a way for finding that creative balance in living. Here are three of them to reflect on. You may know or discover others on your own journey.

The Sabbath

The one everyone will know (but many fail to live out) is the principle of Sabbath rest given in the accounts of creation and in the Ten Commandments:

> Thus the heavens and the earth were finished, and all their multitude. And on the seventh day God finished the work that he had done, and he rested on the seventh day from all the work that he had done. So God blessed the seventh day and hallowed it, because on it God rested from all the work that he had done in creation. (Genesis 2.1-3)

> Remember the sabbath day, and keep it holy. For six days you shall labour and do all your work. But the seventh day is a Sabbath to the Lord your God; you shall not do any work – you, your son or your daughter, your male or female slave, your livestock, or the alien resident in your towns. For in six days the Lord made heaven and earth, the sea, and all that is in them, but rested the seventh day; therefore the Lord blessed the sabbath day and consecrated it. (Exodus 20.8-11; see also Deuteronomy 5.12-15)

According to the ancient theologians who wrote the early parts of Genesis, the principle of rest is woven into the fabric of creation. According to Jesus, God's ordering of the Sabbath in this way is for the good of humanity not simply an arbitrary rule to be kept. Until comparatively recently, this ordering of life around a seven-day week with one day for quiet and rest was written into the fabric and rhythms of our own society. Commercial pressures mean that it is now hard to detect in any but the most superficial ways. There is great virtue and wisdom, however, in seeking to weave a Sabbath pattern into your own life: setting aside at least a day each week for rest, reflection and re-creation, together with longer time and space at intervals through the year. It is not for nothing that these are called holy days. Both the Sabbath and holidays are genuinely times for renewal and perspective on the work that we have been called to do. The society around us may want to live and work 24/7. A Christian is called to dance to a different and slower rhythm.

The gracious shaping of time

> And there was evening and there was morning, the first day. (Genesis 1.5)

In his book, *Working the Angles: The Shape of Pastoral Integrity*, Eugene Peterson draws attention to the way time is shaped according to the first chapter of Genesis and the whole of the Jewish tradition. Ask yourself the simple question: 'When does the day begin?' For most Western Christians, the day begins in the morning when we get up and go to or begin our work and take the world on our shoulders. The evening is the time when we rest from our day's work. We make our contribution (as if the world depends on us) and then, when we have earned it, we take our rest. Again, for the writers of the early chapters of Genesis, there is a different wisdom. The day begins in the evening. For the first half to two-thirds of the day, therefore, most of us are at rest. The world carries on without us (really well) and is still there when we get up the next day. God is sustaining and watching over creation. Life is God's gracious gift to us. Then, part-way through the day, after we have rested and enjoyed creation, we go to work and join in what God is already doing.

This is a way of giving a shape to time which in our present context is deeply counter-cultural. Part of us loves to believe that the world (or the Church) depends on us. It is not wrong to realize that our own contribution can make a difference, but we need to cherish every insight which helps us to realize that we are not at the centre of the universe. All we are called to do is to join in what God is already doing. Realizing that we are resting through the first part of each day before we are called to work is a powerful way of rethinking the pattern of our days. The evening and the morning are the most helpful and natural times for a Christian to pray: as we end our day's work and leave it with God in the evening and as we take it up again the next day.

The Benedictine way: prayer, rest and work

The Rule of Benedict takes these ideas further in seeking to find a way of shaping the day and the week according to what Benedict discerned were true priorities for human living and for fruitfulness over time. Benedict was seeking to give a shape to community life which was genuinely counter-cultural and different from the society around the monastery where other values dominated. Life in the monastery was set by the rhythm of daily prayer. After prayer came proper time for rest and recreation. After rest and recreation came proper time for work. Through ordering life according to these simple principles, Benedict helped to create a way of building human society which was hugely fruitful in terms of its contribution to human civilization (we owe the founding of hospitals, schools and universities to the monastic movement), yet also *good* for those who shared its life.

For parts of your period of training, you may be able to draw on some of this Benedictine ordering of life which still shapes time to some extent for some theological colleges, course residential weekends, parishes, churches and cathedrals.

Some practical guidelines

Establish good habits for time off

When you are facing a life which has multiple demands, one helpful way forward is to draw a line through time off well in advance. If you are to work out the Sabbath principle in practice, you will need the equivalent of at least a clear day off each week. If this simply is not workable in your present pattern of work and study then make this a priority for discussion with your tutor. You will similarly need other parts to the week and to the day which have some space in them.

When our children were younger (writes Steven), the time between five and seven each day was set aside for the routines of feeding, baths and bedtime. Both parents needed to be there to make the time manageable and fun. It wasn't exactly a restful time when we had four children under six, but it was right to make it a priority.

Set clear boundaries around working and study time

Academic work and sermon preparation can be conceived as endless tasks. There is always another book you can read for an essay, always another commentary you can consult before writing a sermon. Unless you put boundaries around certain tasks, they will spread into the rest of your life and take over. You will need to be accountable to someone for keeping those boundaries.

Plan holidays, study weeks and retreats well in advance

Do what you can to anticipate the rhythm of your year during the period of initial training and the early years of recognized ministry. Think carefully about when you will need rest and recreation and when holidays are possible for you – then plan them well in advance.

Establish good boundaries between 'work' and home

It will be important for your own well-being to know when you are working and when you are not, and place will be an important factor in this. It will also be important for family and close friends to know when you can be disturbed and when you are working. These boundaries may not be as clear physically as in a pattern where you went out to work and came home. There will be periods of study at home. You may have to live in a single room in a college setting for much of the year. You may need to study more in your time at home. Thinking through your workspace, the use of libraries, setting aside a particular area for work can all be helpful ways forward.

Build in good patterns of sleep, exercise and diet

Be aware that all of these changes in equilibrium and new places can affect sleep patterns (and that disrupted sleep can begin a cycle of other things changing). New meal times or demands in the mornings and evenings can change your diet which may need to be thought about. Weekends away regularly may mean domestic tasks shift unfairly onto someone else or are simply neglected. If you are spending much of your time studying (essentially a sedentary occupation) then you will probably need to build in more exercise as well.

Family responsibilities

Almost every person in training will have some kind of responsibilities to family: to husband or wife, to young children, to siblings or to elderly parents, to grandchildren, to very close friends who have become like an extended family. The way these family responsibilities are shaped will play a very large part in the way in which life can be balanced (or not) during training. Often they will rightly play a part in discerning how training might be shaped in reality at this particular life stage with this particular set of responsibilities. These factors may govern, for example, whether an older ordinand trains on a course or in a college.

The Bible and the tradition do not contain one simple set of principles on how to balance family responsibilities and the call and demands of ministry. There are many passages which speak of the priority of family life and responsibilities (notably Genesis 2.24-25 and the fifth and seventh commandments). There are other passages, however, particularly in the Gospels, where the call of Jesus and of the kingdom of God is placed above the conventional call and demands of immediate family.

Check it out

Look up the following passages for places where our commitment to our own families is challenged by the words of Jesus:

- Mark 1.19-20   James and John leave their father
- Mark 3.31-35   Jesus and his immediate family
- Mark 10.28-31   Leaving family and possessions for the kingdom
- Luke 9.59-60   'Let me go and bury my father'

There are still other parts of Scripture where the way in which we live out our family lives and commitments is seen as one of the fundamental ways in which Christian ministers witness to God's grace and love:

> Husbands, love your wives, just as Christ loved the church and gave himself up for her. (Ephesians 5.25)

> [I]f someone does not know how to manage his own household, how can he take care of God's church? (1 Timothy 3.5)

Every Christian called to service in the life of the Church will experience at least some tension at some time between their call to Christian ministry and their own family responsibilities. In general and simple terms, the right ordering of these priorities according to Scripture should *not* be seen as:

1. God

2. Ministry

3. Family.

Family responsibilities are to be seen as a vocation which is often prior to a vocation to ministry in time (you were called to be a child, a spouse, a parent, before you were called to ministry), but which also takes priority over a particular work or task in terms of importance. The right, normal ordering of priorities is better seen as:

1. God

2. Family

3. Ministry.

In simple terms, you are irreplaceable as a wife, husband, parent, close family member. You are not irreplaceable in any particular task of ministry. If you find you are beginning to neglect your close family relationships for the sake of the work to which you believe you are called (whether ministry or training for ministry) take a good look at your motives. More often than not, people neglect these close relationships for much less worthy reasons. One person stays up late writing an essay rather than spending time with the family in order to get a really good mark. In reality the person is driven by competition, but this can be disguised as a desire to serve God better. Another person spends every hour available visiting people in need rather than spending time at home. In reality the person is driven by a need to be needed, but this can be disguised as a desire to give yourself to God in ministry. A third person accepts every invitation to serve on committees or to speak at prestigious events to the detriment of their family relationships. In reality the person is driven by ambition, but this can be disguised as putting God first. A fourth pleads pastoral busyness as an excuse for never keeping in touch with close family who live at a distance. Laziness is disguised as obligation.

Marriage and preparation for ministry

These priorities and dilemmas apply to all family relationships. However, the Christian tradition places a particular priority on marriage as a lifelong and particular commitment of mutual support and love. The marriage relationship therefore needs particular and careful consideration in the light of the demands of training.

The understanding of marriage and ministry which has developed in both the Church of England and the Methodist Church is that of husband and wife having separate and individual vocations to work out before God, but also of their being called to lifelong and mutual support of one another's ministries and service. If one partner is called to Christian ministry, it is not even essential that the other partner shares their Christian faith (though this is normally the case). It should not be assumed that if one partner has a vocation to recognized ministry, then the other partner will share in this vocation as an unpaid church worker or pastoral assistant (although a husband or wife may voluntarily embrace this kind of role for a time and find great fulfilment within it). Nor should it be assumed that the life and work of the person called to recognized ministry is somehow more important than or takes priority over the life and work of the person called to be a carer at home or to pursue their vocation as a social worker, a manager, a teacher or as a volunteer outside the churches. A pattern of living needs to be developed which is faithful to the husband and wife's calling to be married, and faithful to the individual calling of each person.

There are a number of particular ways in which the entry to training will raise issues for a husband and wife. Beginning training and finding a new balance will almost always affect both partners very deeply (whether because of extra commitments in the same place, or relocation for training as a family, or living separately for part of each week). This means that, almost certainly, there will be a need for additional time together to work through the implications of this for your relationship (at exactly a time when you may both be coping with extra calls on your time). The second is that the partner in training may well be experiencing all manner of change and growth and new relationships and possibilities. Great care needs to be taken, as at any period of change and growth in a marriage, to keep one another up to date and included in these changes. It will therefore be important to have time and space for conversation and to take up any opportunities for a spouse to share in the life of the training institution (by sharing in meals and worship, parts of residential weekends, social events, etc.). The third is that, almost certainly, the spouse of someone in training for recognized ministry will be thinking through the implications of this for their own life and may also be thinking through their own calling at the same time (in the most general terms of their life's work, purpose and direction). Again, this process will need the support of the partner in training and, often, wisdom and guidance from others.

As a personal example (writes Steven), this book has been written during a time of significant change in my own ministry which has also meant a change for my whole family: relocating to a different city; new schools; new work. Ann, my wife, and I, have attempted to navigate this change better than we have in the past by setting aside a Sunday morning once a month to talk together about all of the different changes and developments and how they are affecting us individually and together.

In the Church of England and the Methodist Church, the training institutions have a responsibility for pastoral care of those in training which extends to their immediate families. It is therefore absolutely appropriate for spouses to draw on the resources of the college or course and for there to be some provision to enable this to take place.

Singles and preparation for ministry

Many people who enter training for ministry are, of course, not married but single: some because they have never been married; others because they have been widowed or divorced. While there are some adjustments in training which are common to all married people, single people vary much more widely in terms of their experience of training, their life stage and the elements in training which may be welcome or difficult. For that reason, we have not been able to develop this issue of balance to the same degree for the different forms of the single life. However, finding ways to sustain key existing relationships and friendships will be vital; so will finding ways to be open to new communities and friendships. The particular ways in which you adjust in these ways to training will, again, need to be the subject for reflection and, possibly, conversation with your own support team.

Be patient with yourself!

No one ever manages the perfect balance of the demands of training for ministry and the rest of life. Give yourself space and time to adjust to the new shape of life and anticipate that energy will need to be given to this and that it will form part of your own reflection by yourself and with others. Continue to make space for that reflection as other changes come along. Take note of how others are handling the changes and learn from them. When you get things wrong, learn from the mistakes but be prepared to forgive yourself and move on. The lives of the prophets, the apostles and the saints down the ages rarely appear to be perfectly balanced. Thankfully, God uses incomplete and imperfect people. But for the sake of those close to you, for your own sake and for the sake of the ministry, give some thought as you go through training to these questions of balance and how to live well in the ministry to which you are called.

Going further

1.   How hard should a minister work? How hard should someone in training work?

2.   Draw up some guidelines for yourself and for others on balancing time during your period of initial training.

Further reading

Colin Buckland, *Liberated to Lead*, Kingsway, 2002.

Chris Edmondson, *Fit to Lead*, Darton, Longman & Todd, 2002.

Gordon MacDonald, *Ordering Your Private World*, Highland, 1984.

Eugene Peterson, *Working the Angles: The Shape of Pastoral Integrity*, Eerdmans, 1982.

Esther de Waal, *A Life-Giving Way*, SPCK, 1995.

8

Learning in transition and community

A church is a community of people who love Jesus and are on a journey together. To travel together is to be changed. Change and community are, therefore, part of the fabric of church life. This chapter looks at these elements in the process of training and formation.

> At the end of the first course residential, John wanted to pack his bags and never come back. He missed his wife and young son terribly. All of the people here were much cleverer than he was. They all talked in a terribly churchy language instead of just speaking of Jesus. The lectures were way above his head – and there was a huge amount of gossip about the staff.
>
> Four weeks into her college course, Sandra was absolutely certain she was in the wrong place. The pace seemed frenetic. She longed for her own house instead of the tiny little room up three flights of stairs. The place was full of evangelical men, some of whom didn't even recognize her call. The worship was dull and the lectures too basic. So far she hadn't made a single friend.

Experiencing this change for yourself and entering into a new community can be very hard. Some of the most valuable learning during your time of training for ministry will not be from textbooks or lectures or even directly from the Scriptures: it will be the learning which happens as you engage with this kind of change honestly along with other Christian people. For that reason, change and community are part of every experience of Christian learning and preparation for ministry. Take them seriously.

The change is made up of change taking place within individuals and change taking place within the training community of a college or course. These individual changes are as varied as people themselves and the circumstances of their lives when they enter training. Some are simply about the events and circumstances of living: the birth of children, falling in love, illness or bereavement. The life of a community in training is affected by all of these individual changes – sometimes very deeply indeed – but it also has its own rhythm.

At the beginning of each new year, normally in September, a large number of new people join the community of learning: typically this can be between a third and a half of the student members of a college or course. The community is literally experiencing re-formation during the early months of its life. Those who were newcomers a year or two years ago are now exercising leadership and responsibility within the group. At the end of the year, again, between one third and half the students in the college or course leave to move on to recognized ministry. For those who remain, there is a sense also of letting go, of moving on and preparing to welcome a new group of students in a few months time. Whether your training is course or college based, the relationships which are formed through shared worship, prayer, meals, learning and relaxation together have the potential to be deep and long lasting.

These elements of change and community form such a rich source of learning for understanding and serving the Church because churches also are communities where individuals are experiencing change and which have their own dynamic of journey and moving on. Any church congregation, of course, is experiencing the full range of changes which are brought about simply by living life: illness and bereavement, love and new beginnings. A church congregation will have those who are coming into membership either through moving into a new area as Christians (and therefore experiencing all kinds of transitions) or those who are coming to faith for the first time (which is all about being transformed). The same congregation will also experience people moving on to new jobs, ministries and areas; going to university; moving out of the area; or, sadly, drifting away from faith and worship or leaving in anger and disappointment.

In most contexts there will also be a wider picture of gradual change and transition whether that change is simply reactive (the scenario of steady decline and diminishing resources) or proactive (the scenario of intentional renewal of worship and mission and the growth of the congregation). A key part of the leadership skills necessary for all in recognized ministry is understanding these dynamics of change and community. Learning about them in lectures or books is one thing – learning through living them out in a formational community is another.

The first part of the chapter looks at how individuals are affected by a transition into a new community. Think about it in relation to your own experience in beginning training for ministry, but also in relation to beginning ministry in a new situation or joining a church. The second looks at how communities are formed; and the third at some principles and resources for community learning and community life.

Elements in transition

In my early years of working in theological education (writes Steven), I needed to learn how to help a new community form well at the beginning of each year and how to help individuals move through what in a college setting is a very rapid and deep process of transition. The material which follows emerged directly from listening to these stories and elements in the change and has been tried and tested over the years. The changes may be less marked if your context for training is a course (as in most cases some elements in your life remain the same), but the same four factors are likely to be present.

Expectations

Everyone enters training with a set of expectations about what it will be like. These expectations have been formed in a whole range of ways. Some are formed by good-natured advice given by family and friends: 'Make sure you don't lose your faith when you go on that course!' Some are formed by other experiences of Christian community: 'I thought the summer school would be like Spring Harvest and the residentials like the parish weekend.' Other expectations, rightly, are shaped by talking to students already in the programme, through impressions formed at interview, and by information provided in advance. In one sense this whole book is about helping to shape appropriate expectations so that you get the most from your training.

All of these ingredients – and our own hopes and fears and personality – mean that before you begin the new course you have a picture or a map in your head about what things will be like. Think of your own map for a moment and then reflect that one thing is absolutely guaranteed: there is *certain* to be some mismatch between expectation and reality. Your map will not be 100 per cent accurate (or anything like it). Therefore a process of adjustment will be taking place within every individual in the first year of a new programme of study.

There are two possible ways in which this adjustment can happen. One works and the other, generally, does not. The first is to take a long hard look at the reality, realize it does not match the map and redraw the map accordingly. The second is to compare the two and seek to adjust reality to your own ideas of what it should be like. The person who adopts the first view is well on the way to gaining a great deal from their college or course experience. The person who takes the second is likely to spend their time in college or on the course attempting to change as much as possible (and therefore not learning as much as they might). A new student once presented us with a list of five ways to change the life of the college four weeks in advance of his first term.

In the early period of this kind of transition, what might seem to others to be small things may assume a disproportionate size and stir up a surprising amount of anger and disappointment until trust can grow between the individual and the institution.

The first evening of lectures on the course overran by 20 minutes. John missed his train home and he and his wife had an enormous row. He assumed that the whole course would now be marked by sloppy timekeeping. His wife assumed that she was in for three years of her husband not keeping his promises and coming home late. John sat down and wrote a furious letter of complaint to the principal. In fact, there had been a simple confusion about times between the principal and the new guest lecturer. This was the only time a session had overrun in the course of the last year.

Sue – a single Methodist student – arrived for her first worship service at the college, which was all-age worship. The service was very Anglican in form and full of little children running around seemingly out of control. She assumed from this first experience that all of college life would be like this: centred around young families and not acknowledging her own tradition. She had a sleepless night and by breakfast the next morning was ready to pack her bags and leave. In fact this would be the only all-age worship for that term and two days later there was a Methodist service for the whole community.

Mismatched expectations work, of course, in a positive as well as a negative way. There are many ways in which those in training find a particular course exceeds their expectations: the learning and community are much richer than they ever imagined possible. However, our experience suggests that in the first few months it is the disappointments rather than the joys which are most likely to surface.

Training institutions help students to adjust in transition in different ways:

- By attempting to present themselves in a way that matches reality as much as possible (e.g., in not promising what cannot be delivered).

- Through patient and non-defensive listening when people have difficult first reactions to things.

- Through apologizing honestly when things go wrong (as they do, even in the best of institutions).

- Through being committed to continuous change and improvement.

A helpful and positive modelling of these things by the institution is a powerful learning experience for those who will go on to put the same elements in place within the life of a local church.

Loss

If you are moving to theological college this almost always involves loss: of proximity to friends and close family; possibly of status and a job you have enjoyed; of a telephone, a desk, a secretary and an office; of a higher income; of a title and place within an institution; usually of an active and fruitful ministry in a local church; and of a network of relationships and leisure activities which, for most people, has been a settled pattern. Beginning a course of part-time study normally involves loss of some kind as well: of some free time and energy; laying down areas of ministry in the local church, and so on.

Most people would acknowledge that there are gains as well as losses in the changes and that, in the context of their vocation, the gain is the greater. However, the way loss affects us is varied and unpredictable; we may have bad days on which we might be tempted to project 'blame' for the loss we are experiencing onto the institution or onto God. The degree to which this affects us is likely to be linked not only to what we have lost but also to how we have dealt with other bereavement and loss in recent years.

We are all helped to move through periods of loss by recognizing what is happening and by being listened to. Clearly we will be helped most therefore by those with whom we have been friends for many years and who can help us reflect on the new situation. Again, this is more straightforward for those who are training in a place where they have lived for many years (although time with close friends may be squeezed by additional demands). In time, however, we also need to establish new and supportive relationships within the training context: to have people we trust in the learning environment as well. As with any loss, as we acknowledge the reality so we are able to grieve honestly and, in time, to move forward.

Steven writes: my own most profound period of loss and bereavement in ministry (so far) was leaving the parish where I had been vicar for nine years to take up my post as warden of Cranmer Hall. The time in the parish had been deeply formational; two of our children had been born there; we had been extremely happy as a family. The experience is crystallized for me in the memory of driving away from the vicarage after the removal van had left. We chose a route that took us out past the local school and the church. My wife and our children were in tears. The first two years of learning to do my new job were also years, for the whole family, of acknowledging what we had lost and adjusting to that loss in appropriate ways.

Culture

Communities of formation, just like churches, have their own culture. That culture may not be obvious even to those within them: it may be summed up in a whole host of different customs and roles and ways of relating to one another which are not written down but passed on in scores of subtle ways. Some training institutions have a strong culture of welcome and are easy to be part of. Some have a strong culture of hierarchy with a clear order of who is important and who is not. In some, there is a strong Anglican ethos which is far more obvious to those from other traditions than it is to the Anglicans. In the same way in some churches newcomers are asked to take on significant tasks on their second Sunday. In others, you may need to be a regular worshipper for six years before you are asked to join the coffee rota.

The move from previous context to course or college may involve a number of changes of culture:

- For some it may be a transition from a working-class to a more middle-class culture for the first time.

- For others there may be a marked transition from sitting on the edge of church life to becoming part of Church as institution – which may not be welcome.

- For still others there is a culture shift from a work environment to one of higher education.

Increasingly, as patterns of training change, more people will take different parts of their training within different institutions and so may experience this culture change part-way through their learning. Some will be able to handle the cultural transition well and gradually. Others students, spouses or staff may experience profound culture shock in which one common and understandable response is to want to change the culture into which one is coming or else to run away from what is unfamiliar.

Reflection on this process of cultural adjustment is vital and a necessary part of the training and learning process. You will experience similar times of transition in the future and be involved in helping others enter the different culture of a local church.

Important too are the provision of accurate maps, guides and induction.

Confusion

The fourth element of transition is simply one of confusion in a new environment, with a great deal of new information which needs to be processed. Moreover the very environment is one of learning in which presuppositions and cherished ideas and beliefs are to be challenged and discussed almost from the first day. At a deeper level too there may be confusion (or at least a lack of a common understanding) about what people are being trained to do and how that training is effective.

Be patient with yourself and with others as you navigate through this confusion. It is very embarrassing to turn up in the wrong place at the wrong time for a meeting or a lecture (particularly if people don't yet know you), but it is completely *normal* for someone passing through a time of significant change. Our minds can only process so much new information at a time – particularly as we grow older. Eventually we go into overload and something gives. Over time, we do assimilate the information and the new rhythms of learning and training become second nature.

Opportunities and dangers in transition

There are significant opportunities for growth and the grace of God in a time of transition. A time of change in outward circumstances offers the opportunity for deep inner transformation and change: deep-set attitudes and ideas are questioned; tested and sometimes transformed in the process of adjusting to a new environment. As some supports are being taken away, we can be helped in developing our dependence upon God and a healthy interdependence in our relationships with others. We see ourselves more clearly (and uncomfortably) reflected in a new environment. We have the opportunity to grow towards a deeper maturity. However, there are also some dangers.

In a difficult transition to training, expectations about college may not be met; you may experience an acute sense of loss; it may be your first experience of transition to a different culture; there may be a great deal of confusion about what is required and why. As a result, you may begin to find yourself not responding at all well to your training institution. You may attempt to change things before that is appropriate, or pick out areas of weakness and judge that the whole thing has gone wrong. You might withdraw; you might even start to regress or react angrily to what is happening. You may lose confidence in yourself and in your calling and gifts. There are very few new students or staff members in a training institution who do not experience at least some of these things in their first few terms.

'Deskilling'

This temporary loss of confidence and taking time to adjust to a new situation is sometimes described by those who experience it as being 'deskilled'. What is meant here is usually a combination of feeling that gifts and skills you have exercised previously in ministry (and which have been an important part of your own identity) may not be immediately recognized or used within the training context. As a result of that you find it harder to be yourself and to find your place within the new situation and, understandably, there is some temporary loss of confidence and self-esteem.

However, we have learned to be cautious about using the term 'deskilling' for this transitional experience. There is need for a more robust view of gifts and skills here: if you genuinely have these abilities they will not be lost or diminished through not using them for a few weeks or months. In any healthy community, over time, there will be an opportunity for most people to use their gifts or to discover new ones as part of the learning process and people will, in time, get to know you (providing you are willing to share something of yourself). For most people all of these experiences are a temporary phase and part of the process of change.

However, if the community is not a healthy one for you (as sometimes happens) or if you do not allow people to get to know you or navigate transition well, then this temporary loss of confidence may become permanent. In that case a person may genuinely find that they have been deskilled and not empowered through entry into the training process. For that reason, careful navigation of entry into training is vital.

Guides in transition

Over time, in Cranmer Hall and the Wesley Study Centre, we have developed the following guidelines for students through the initial months of training, and they all apply in a range of different training contexts:

- Recognize what is happening and the realities of transition.

- Make full use of your tutor and other course or college resources.

- Take time in the early months to build strong networks of relationships.

- Try and have some aspects of your environment which give continuity.

- Don't feel you have to accept the course or college culture as the 'only' culture (a much more common thing in a college).

- Ensure that there are some people in this environment who know and appreciate your gifts, talents and past history.

How does community form?

Intentional formation of community

Christian community forms in any context as people come together with a common purpose and begin to share their lives. It rarely happens by accident: it is quite possible for a group of individuals to take the same courses at the same time and never become community. In a training context community is formed *intentionally*: the way the training is shaped helps people to get to know one another.

There are a number of ways of describing the formation of community. They apply to the way community happens in small groups (whether home groups or nurture groups) and in teams, as well as in large contexts. It helps both to understand the process as a linear development (although of course it is never as neat as this) and to be aware of a number of other factors which shape community living.

The formation of community can be a reality for a group of people meeting for evening lectures and the occasional Saturday or weekend away, providing time for building a common life is built into the programme. In a college situation, the same kind of care is needed: just because people spend a lot of time in the same building does not mean that they become community.

The following picture gives an overview of the linear development of a group of strangers to the goal of Christian fellowship and community described by the Greek word *koinonia* (usually translated *fellowship* in the New Testament):

Strangers

Storytelling

Affirmation/Conflict

Task/Force

Koinonia

The different stages should not be understood as neatly divided but as overlapping. Getting to 'first base' for a group of strangers is normally about creating an opportunity to tell your story and to listen to the stories of other people. Clearly this needs to happen imaginatively and helpfully: for a group of 25 each to listen to a half-hour narrative of one another's lives would be unmanageable. However, for all small groups, to miss out this stage and move straight on to undertaking some task together normally leads to difficulties. Anyone leading a group needs to allow time and space in agendas and meeting time for this intentional telling of the story. The depth of sharing and disclosure is normally set by those responsible for leading the group.

Any group of people who begin to share in this way will find in time that there are things they want to affirm about one another and areas where there is potential conflict. In order for the group to work together well, the ability to deal with both of these areas in a safe way is essential. As people share their stories and begin to engage with a common task, this kind of affirmation and difference begins to emerge and is normally a sign of healthy development in the life of the group. Again, it needs time and space as relationships deepen.

Finally, in order to have the opportunity to develop to maturity, any group needs a common task or an external focus. Christian community at its heart is not inward looking but outward facing. We learn a certain amount about one another by sitting face to face and talking (and this is necessary). However, we learn so much more by working side by side – whether that is painting a fence, leading a service, or cooking a meal. Out of these three elements of sharing ourselves, being able to affirm or disagree with one another and working together emerge the gift of community, of Christian fellowship.

Part of the pattern developed in Durham is to allow good time in the first term of the year for a new group of students to share different aspects of their stories (through an induction course) and to reflect on aspects of their working life together (through a course on theological and practical reflection). In the second term the whole group goes away together for a first-year weekend of outdoor activities and team building, working in a number of smaller groups. Affirmation and conflict begin to be expressed in that (normally safe) setting. Students then work together for the rest of the year in these small groups and lead a circuit/parish mission together in June as part of a two-week course in evangelism and nurture.

Prayer, meals and modelling

This intentional formation of community is undergirded, supported and enabled by three other essential elements in any context. All are deeply rooted in the Scriptures, particularly in the Gospels, and in the whole of the Christian tradition. Common prayer is seen as foundational to Christian community. Prayers and worship in the context of evenings, weekends or a college term should therefore not be seen simply as an element in training and preparation for the ministry which will follow (in which case the emphasis might be on exposing students to a wide range of different materials and good practice). They are also about enabling a diverse range of people to share a common life grounded in worship and prayer in the present. Shaping worship to balance these two different needs is never easy. However, it seems to us that the worshipping needs of the present community take priority.

Shared meals and time together which is not structured or part of the curriculum is, of course, vital to building friendships and relationships. This is provided both through meals which are offered by the course or college but also through informal times and Christian people naturally offering hospitality to one another. Modelling community and good practice in the formation of community is the responsibility not simply of the core staff team but of all Christian disciples and Christian ministers (which means in this context *you* as much as anybody else).

Staff and students learning together

A vital part of the creation of Christian community in a training context is the combining of staff and students into a common Christian enterprise in which people are first and foremost disciples of Jesus Christ and only then live out their different roles in relation to the process of formation. Kindness, courtesy and charity are vital elements in the creation of this kind of community. So too is mutuality: the openness of both staff and students to give and receive encouragement and support, advice and help. Vital too is the realization that for the staff members (and even for visiting lecturers) the encounter with this community is a time of formation and development sometimes in an even more powerful way than for the students in training.

Resources and guidelines for community living

Scripture and tradition are huge resources for Christian living. Within the Scriptures, give due priority to the Gospels and to the pattern of shared life worked out by Jesus and the disciples. Jesus' words in Matthew 18 on the common life among the disciples are very significant for communities of formation. There is clear teaching here on the importance of welcome, of humility, of due care for one another, especially for the vulnerable and those who are drifting away. The chapter gives guidelines for the handling of conflict, complaint and disagreement in community:

> If another member of the church sins against you, go and point out the fault when the two of you are alone. If the member listens to you, you have regained that one. But if you are not listened to, take one or two others along with you, so that every word may be confirmed by the evidence of two or three witnesses. If the member refuses to listen to them, tell it to the church; and if the offender refuses to listen even to the church, let such a one be to you as a Gentile and a tax-collector. (Matthew 18.15-17)

and also on forgiveness:

> Then Peter came and said to him, 'Lord, if another member of the church sins against me, how often should I forgive? As many as seven times?' Jesus said to him, 'Not seven times, but, I tell you, seventy-seven times.' (Matthew 18.21-22)

The verses need to be interpreted with care, like all of Scripture. However, the difficulties with these passages are not so much that they are hard to understand, but that they can be even more difficult to put into practice in a formational community.

The Christian tradition has a rich seam to mine on resources for community living, all drawing on the biblical foundation. We have referred elsewhere to the wisdom carried by the Rule of Benedict. Among contemporary writings on community, the reader is referred to the modern classic by Jean Vanier, founder of the L'Arche Communities, *Community and Growth*. Vanier concludes his work with these paragraphs on the purpose and nature of true Christian community:

Community life is there to help us, not to flee from our deep wound [of isolation] but to remain within the reality of love. It is there to help us believe that our illusions and egoism will be gradually healed if we become nourishment for others. We are in community for each other, so that all of us can grow and uncover our wound before the infinite, so that Jesus can manifest himself through it.

But we can only accept our own deep wound when we have discovered that community is a place where our heart can put down roots, a place where we are at home. The roots are not there to comfort us, or turn us in on ourselves. Quite the opposite: they are there so that each of us can grow and bear fruit for humanity and for God. We put down roots when we discover the covenant among people who are called to live together, and the covenant with God and with the poor. Community is not there for itself but for others – the poor, the Church and society. It is essentially mission.[1]

Going further

1.   What do you think are the main changes ahead for you in the next year? What resources are there for you to address those changes?

2.   Describe the best experience you have had of Christian community. What made it so good? What did you learn for the future?

Further reading

Dietrich Bonhoeffer, *Life Together*, SCM Press, 1954.

Steven Croft, *Transforming Communities*, Darton, Longman & Todd, 2002.

Jean Vanier, *Community and Growth*, revised edition, Darton, Longman & Todd, 1989.

Part Three: Understanding and serving the Church

9

Learning about your own Church and other Churches

Imagine you are in a meeting of people you don't know well or have not met before. Perhaps you are on a conference, a training day, the first day of a new job or the first meeting of a local community group. It is suggested that it would be good for everyone to introduce himself or herself and you are asked go first. What do you say?

Well, you would probably say your name. After that you could add number of different things. Depending on context you might say something about where you live and or where you grew up, your age, whether you are married and have children, what work you do or have done in life, what your hobbies are, where you go to church, and what led you to be at this meeting.

Whatever you choose to say you will be sharing something not only about yourself but also about your past. Even if it is only your name you share, you are revealing to people the name that your parents chose for you or, in some cases, a name you chose for yourself in the past. Your name may be an English, Welsh, Indian or Chinese name, which means that you have links with certain parts of the world. It may have a long history in your family (our daughter's Christian name was also the name of my grandmother), or it may have been given to you for some other particular reason (to cite an obvious example, David and Victoria Beckham's son was called Brooklyn because he was conceived when they stayed in New York). Equally many surnames indicate something about that family's location or occupation in the distant past. Whether you are conscious of it or not, your name carries a history and indicates some of the things that have shaped your life. Adding other information to your introduction will simply add other elements that have shaped you and thus are now part of your identity.

All of us are fashioned by the geography, history and events of our lives and those that went before us. In faith terms when we come to preparation for ministry we come from a particular Christian tradition and we will have been formed by it. We probably know something about that tradition and how we have been shaped by it but, as with our names, there are most probably parts of the story that we do not know.

In this chapter we will attempt to sketch out what learning about your own and other people's Church traditions might look like, point to some aspects of the learning that need careful attention, and suggest ways of getting the most from the enterprise.

Reasons for exploring our own tradition

As suggested above, one reason for learning about our own Church tradition is that it helps us understand who we are and how we have been shaped by the tradition to which we belong. There are other reasons too.

Learning about our own tradition helps us to understand how and where we fit into the broader scheme of things. Some traditions have grown out of others, for example, Methodism from the Church of England. Some have arisen as a reaction to other traditions or aspects of them. The Lutheran Church is, in one sense at least, a reaction to medieval Roman Catholicism. Other Christian traditions have developed in different ways for geographical and linguistic reasons. Examples might be the Armenian and Coptic Churches, compared with the Eastern Orthodox, or some of the indigenous African Christian Churches. Having some sense of how the different denominations came to be and how we relate to each other can help us discover our common heritage and, even where we differ, help us to work together more effectively.

A third reason for such a study of our own tradition is to explore what our Church needs in terms of ministry. Although some people talk about 'my ministry' or 'my calling' as if it were simply a direct arrangement between the person and God, ministry is in reality the ministry of the Church, as an expression of being the body of Christ. The Church's ministry is an expression of its self-understanding and calling. Each tradition needs women and men who can further its work by ministering in ways that are resonant with its ethos and vocation. Learning about one's own tradition means discovering how the Church's ministry is linked to its history, theology and spirituality, in order to see what is required and how you can best be a minister within such a Church.

At the same time no Church or tradition stands still. We are called to serve the present age and proclaim the good news afresh for our generation. Understanding therefore what has shaped our tradition and what it holds as precious may allow us to know better how to carry forward its life and work. In other words, learning about our own tradition enables us to be discerning about what is central and what is secondary or peripheral. This can helps us in practical ministry when we are unsure how to proceed or what decisions to make. If we are aware of our own tradition at these points, we are in a better position to move forward in ways that are both faithful and innovative.

Reasons for exploring other people's traditions

OK, there may be a good case for studying one's own tradition, but why do you need to understand other Christian traditions?

We have mentioned some of the reasons above. Understanding how we fit in with other traditions helps us understand ourselves, understand others and therefore work with each other better for Christ's kingdom. This is vital today, for the context in which we minister will be an ecumenical one where we will work alongside those from different traditions.

Ecumenical comes from the Greek word *oikoumenē* which means 'whole inhabited earth'. In the early Church, Ecumenical Councils were called so that churches from all parts of the world could be in conversation together.

This has been developing for many years. In part it reflects the ways the Churches have been in closer conversation and partnership in mission and ministry for the last century. Churches in the United Kingdom began serious discussions in the early part of the twentieth century about how to respond to each other in the light of the prayer of Jesus in John 17 that 'they may be one'. Various schemes of church unity were explored resulting, for example, in the forming of the United Reformed Church in 1972. The first Local Ecumenical Partnerships (LEPs) were established in 1964, though in those days they were called Areas of Ecumenical Experiment! By 2004 there were 1,000 LEPs in Britain. In addition, almost every area, town or village has a Churches Together or its equivalent, through which churches have contact, exchange information and often make plans for joint initiatives. Wherever you minister in the life of the Church, you will do so in the context of other Christian Churches and traditions. While each Church, parish or circuit needs to address its own mission, it is profoundly un-Christian to do so without awareness of or consideration for local brothers and sisters in Christ.

At the same time, Christians are far more likely to change Churches now than ever before. When people move to a new area, they may well shop around for a church which suits them rather than attend the church of a denomination to which they belonged previously, or they may simply opt for their nearest church whatever the label. In is not uncommon to find people who have worshipped for a period of their lives in Methodist, Anglican, Baptist and URC settings. While their allegiance to denomination is not a primary consideration in their worship, they may well have experience of several Church structures and patterns of worship. Being aware of these traditions will help you minister to them.

So exploring other people's traditions can make us better able to work with, help and support those who are different from us but who share the same calling to follow Jesus and serve him in the world.

It is also part of our calling to express the unity Christ gives to the Church. One of the central convictions of the New Testament is that God has acted in Jesus to break down barriers and unite those who were formerly divided or excluded. This gift of unity from God needs to be safeguarded for it is part of our message to the world about Jesus. The modern ecumenical movement has been occupied with how best to demonstrate the unity we have in Christ.

Check it out

Read the following passages:
- I Corinthians 12.4-12
- Ephesians 2.11-22; 4.1-7
- John 17 (notice v. 22)
- Galatians 3.26-29

What do you think is meant by unity and why is it important?

Finally, looking at other people's traditions can not only help us value our tradition but occasionally point up some of the weaknesses of our own tradition. In Methodism, for example, there is a strong emphasis on grace, salvation and holiness. This can be found in the sermons of John Wesley and the hymns of Charles Wesley. Neither has a lot to say about the God as creator however, mainly because it was already part of the Anglican tradition and other earlier traditions they could draw on. When Methodists became separate they need to address this weakness. Look in the section entitled 'God's creating and sustaining power' in *Hymns & Psalms* (the hymn book authorized by the Methodist Conference) and notice there are no hymns by Charles Wesley, only one translation by John Wesley but three by Isaac Watts. All traditions need to be aware of their strengths and weaknesses in order to recognize that we need each other.

Pause for thought

How would describe your own Church tradition? Look at the following words and phrases and choose three which you think describe your tradition:

African	Calvinist	Cross-centred
Anglican	Charismatic	Evangelical
Armenian	Congregational	Forward in Faith
Baptist	Conservative	Free-thinking
Bible-preaching	Contemplative	High church

Inclusive	Mission-centred	Reformed
Independent	Non-denominational	Sacramental
Initiated	Pentecostal	Spirit-led
Liberal	Presbyterian	United Reformed Church
Methodist	Radical	

What words are missing from the list that you would want to add?

What might exploring my Church traditions involve?

There are a few things that can be learned from the exercise above.

First, you will see it is possible to identify your tradition in different ways. You may pick a denominational label, a theological emphasis and a form of churchmanship. For example you could identify yourself as a 'Calvinist – Sacramental – Anglican' or 'Evangelical – Charismatic – URC'. Thus there may be different types of Methodist or Anglican or Baptist. Within the Church of England, for example, the high Church tradition contrasts strongly with the evangelical strand. The United Reformed Church has in its recent history the merging of practices from Presbyterian, Congregationalist and Church of Christ traditions. Older members of the Methodist Church may tell you that they were (sometimes still are) Primitive or Wesleyan, even though the two streams came together in 1932! Studying your own tradition will therefore involve not only looking at denominational history and theology but also exploring different streams within those denominations.

Second, choosing some of the words in the list might reveal something about your personal temperament or spirituality. For example, you might identify your tradition as 'Contemplative – Spirit-led – Cross-centred'. While you may have developed this understanding of your tradition within a particular church, others from other denominations and churches may also share it. This might be through the influence of a movement that has affected many denominations such as the charismatic movement or more generally because older patterns of Christian spirituality tend to recur in a whole variety of churches. In order to understand ourselves better and what draws us into certain ways of prayer, worship and service, we may need to look at the roots of these spiritualities.

Third, you might have perceived some of the words as pejorative, words you might only use to describe what you are not! For some the words 'conservative' or 'liberal' or 'evangelical' have a connotation of disapproval. This should alert us to the fact that we sometimes define ourselves over against others and the way we describe other traditions may be by using words that for us are negative or

mischievous. The Anglican–Methodist Covenant Report drew attention to
fact that in the relations between Methodists and Anglicans over nearly three
centuries we have often told the story of the other Church in negative terms, in
order to tell our own story all the more positively. The report suggested that the
first step in growing together would be to acknowledge these negative
descriptions and repent of the harm they have done.

If we are going to understand other people's traditions and want them to
understand ours, we need to engage with them in ways that seek to understand
and appreciate rather than to find easy ways to dismiss that which is different or
unknown.

Finally, you might have been frustrated by the exercise because it was difficult to
describe adequately with three words your own Church tradition. What is more,
some of the words were ambiguous and you might have felt that you needed to
explain more what you meant. This should alert us to the fact that Church
traditions are often complex and variegated and need some degree of patience
to appreciate. We need to get beneath the labels to the reality behind them.

How do courses and programmes help you to explore Church traditions?

Programmes are often places where different traditions meet. In many places
preparation for ministry is deliberately ecumenical. The programmes are designed
for people from and training for ministry in different denominations. The staff
may well be appointed not only to bring different expertise, but also to provide
resources from different Churches and traditions and to support students from
different backgrounds. Colleges often work in partnerships or federations with
colleges of different traditions and share staff resources for teaching and tutorial
work, for the same reasons. Thus students and staff may be from different traditions
and mixing will allow for informal conversations as well as formal teaching.

The approach may be implicit or explicit. Implicit approaches will include
experiencing prayer, worship and study alongside people of different traditions
and allowing the conversation and discussion to arise out of the experience.
Explicit elements may include attention to different traditions within courses or
modules, for example, a discussion of different patterns and views of liturgy, or a
course specifically addressed to denominational traditions such as a module on
Anglicanism.

Somewhere in-between the implicit and explicit is the role of placement,
attachments or 'fieldwork' in a variety of different settings. A student who is from
an evangelical tradition may gain as much from being attached to a 'high church'

parish for a time as an 'evangelical' one. A Methodist local preacher and Anglican lay Reader training alongside each may accompany one another for feedback on sermon construction and delivery, and in the process learn about preaching in different contexts, both physical and liturgical.

Our view is that all these approaches are needed for deep learning, the development of sensitivity in ministry and to enable creative cooperation and development in the Church's life and mission. Being alongside people of other traditions in lectures and seminars and sharing in the worship of other traditions enables you to see and sense convictions and differences. Entering traditions other than your own via placements enables you to identify your own key questions. Addressing the tradition in depth allows you to understand why different emphases and practices arose and why they continue to be important.

The right attitude

How much you learn in this area, like any other, depends on the attitude with which you undertake the exploration as well as the support available for teaching, reflection and discussion. If you enter it with the view that there is nothing to learn, you will probably find your expectation fulfilled. If you have decided that some of the other Christian traditions are suspect or 'of the devil' before you start it will prove hard to engage with them. If on the other hand, you begin with the view that your own tradition is good and valuable and thus is worthy of deeper study, and if you assume that other traditions are to be respected and may have important insights, then it is likely that you will learn much, will be stronger within your tradition and more useful to God's wider purpose.

Here are a few additional tips for getting started on exploring Church tradition.

Make use of your existing knowledge and experience

Don't assume that you know nothing of your own tradition because you are in a formal learning setting where there may be 'experts'. That you are without any knowledge of your Church tradition is highly unlikely, perhaps impossible. You will have been worshipping in your Church for some time, you will have been chosen or supported to explore the avenue of ministry for which you are training and thus you will have engaged with two of the key parts of your Church tradition – its liturgical life and its decision-making structures. Thus you will have built up knowledge of your tradition by being a participating member of it. What is more, this tacit knowledge will be larger than you think. As Michael Polanyi has argued, most people are unaware of how much they know because it is held in an intuitive way. Knowledge is absorbed simply by people being involved in the life of an institution. Hence, most people have the occasional experience of coming out of a seminar with a feeling that the lecturer or another student expressed well what they already knew but could not have articulated. An important part of learning about your own tradition will be relating what you know already to the historical and theological knowledge with which you are presented.

Make use of the experience and insight of others

Like you, others will know things. Fellow students as well as tutors and teaching staff will have things to share and may be able to answer questions for you. Ask the questions that occur to you. Remember that there are no stupid questions, only questions. But don't expect every person from a particular tradition to be an expert – they may be exploring their own tradition like you. We have a memory of an outside lecturer invited to teach a mixed group of Anglican and Methodist students about funeral liturgies. The small number of Methodists in the class listened to the teacher explain the changing pattern of liturgies in the Church of England over time and the reasons for these changes. She then said to the Methodist students, 'Now, you will know all about your services, tell us about them.' Suddenly, they found they had to speak on behalf of their own Church tradition without the study and expert help that she was offering to the others! Their experience of funeral services was limited to the one or two which members had attended as mourners and no one in group had ever studied the words of funeral liturgies in *The Methodist Worship Book* in any detail, let alone its predecessors. Being cast as experts was both disturbing and dangerous. They needed help too.

Begin with respect

Assume that both your tradition and those of others are worthy of respect. *Respect* here is a better word than *tolerance*. *Tolerance* has the sense of a passive, perhaps even grudging, accepting of difference. The word *respect* has an active feel, conveying the idea that traditions carry valuable truth worth knowing. From a basic attitude of respect it is possible to develop empathy and suspend premature judgement in order to make sense of a tradition within its own context. This does not mean that you have to agree with other people's tradition or even parts of your own. Neither does it mean that you cannot challenge other people's practices or convictions. When based on respect, such disagreements and challenges are far more likely to taken seriously by others.

Archbishop Rowan Williams offered a metaphor when he visited the Methodist Conference in 2004. He said the gospel is like a banquet to which you have been invited. There is no reason why you should be invited other than the generosity of the host. You accept and go to the feast, but when you get there the first thing you notice is that there are lots of guests there that you would never have invited. You cannot understand why anyone and especially this host should invite them. Then you remember that there was no good reason why you should be invited either, other than that the host wants you be there. At this point you make a connection. If the host loves, respects and invites everyone there, then surely a measure of respect from you would be appropriate and a willingness to find more about the other guests may help you to understand and respond positively to this generous host. Our respect for other traditions is thus rooted in a view of God's love and grace.

Live with the tension

Working with any group of people who have deeply held convictions, some of them different from our own, creates tension. It is easy to step on other people's toes and easy to feel offended by what you perceive as the insensitive words or actions of others. You see these as disrespectful to your view or Church tradition or just plain wrong! Whenever there is such tension it manifests itself somehow. Our experience is that it is often most keenly felt in worship. Some of the strongest reactions among students (and sometimes staff) are in relation to encountering the worship of other traditions. Equally, developing a worship life with the people with whom you train is a challenge because it must bring together many different strands. Sometimes this can feel very alien to some or all of the participants, as you seek to find ways to represent and honour the different streams present.

This tension need not be negative. Indeed it can be in this tension that growth and movement can occur. The human body is able to work effectively because of tension. Without the tension between different muscles your arms or legs would not move. It is because there is the right level of tension that we can function. Facing tension, naming it and seeking to live within it with both conviction and respect can help prepare you for ministry in a profound way.

Encounters on the way

Like Pilgrim in John Bunyan's story, you are likely to meet some situations and characters on the way through this exploration of Church traditions. Here are some aspects of studying your own tradition that you need to face along the way.

Myths

The word *myth* is in the vocabulary of theological education and it has a technical sense. Where popular use of the word may mean false or untrue, in our context (and other areas of academic study) *myth* means stories or accounts that carry important truth, insight or value, but which may be historically uncertain. For example, Methodists often pride themselves on the 'open table' of communion. This means the invitation to share communion is open to all and the sharing of bread and wine is often prefaced by such words as 'All who love the Lord Jesus and want to follow him are welcome to share in this sacrament.' Many Methodists assume that John Wesley instituted this practice and some even attribute the words of invitation to him. Neither of these ideas is true in fact. However, John Wesley did talk about communion being a 'converting ordinance', meaning that people might experience grace and come to faith through communion. He was also strongly committed to the belief that God's love was for all without exception, in opposition to some of his Calvinist contemporaries. Hence the 'open table' is consistent with his theology, though the practice was a later development; and the myth carries these central convictions in an easily communicable form.

Coming to terms with the main myths of our tradition is important. They help us identify how at a popular level the values and convictions of our tradition are focused and passed on. They also allow us to look at the underlying truths or values and discuss how these are to be expressed and developed for today.

Lost traditions

There is a moving account in 2 Kings 22 of the young King Josiah discovering almost accidentally a lost book of the law. The way he reacts when the recovered book is read shows what impact recovering a lost tradition can have. It certainly had implications for the whole of Josiah's kingdom.

Check it out

Read 2 Kings 22.1-20

We said in Chapter 4 that the Christian tradition is vast, like a mountain range. Even within a single denominational tradition there is a large and complex history and it is easy for whole parts of the tradition to be lost for a time. Part of exploring one's own tradition is beginning to discover the scope of what has formed a particular Church tradition. The Church of England, for example, has been formed by the particularities of Henry VIII's England, the Reformation, the thinking and writing of Richard Hooker, the prayer book of Thomas Cranmer, the Stuarts, the Puritans and Oliver Cromwell, the missionary enterprises and the Tractarians of the nineteenth century, the Lambeth Conference, and many influential scholars, poets, church leaders and innovators such as George Herbert, Charles Simeon, F. D. Maurice, William Temple, as well as through the Church of England's relationships with other Church traditions such as the Church of Rome, the English Dissenters and the Methodists. This is a rich and varied tradition, and often the leaders of one period or strand of the Church's life have claimed that they were recovering parts of the tradition that had gone before and been forgotten.

Likewise, Methodists are often surprised to discover how sacramental in emphasis were John and Charles Wesley. Nineteenth-century developments in the Methodist Church moved away from the emphasis on communion, but the founders of the movement urged weekly communion and published a book of hymns specifically for use at the Lord's Supper. In the late 1960s when Roman Catholics and Methodist theologians met for one of their regular discussion they looked at these early Methodist hymns and the Roman Catholic theologians became excited at the range and depth of theology in them. Ironically at this time Methodists in Britain celebrated communion once a quarter, usually after the main morning service, and rarely if ever sang hymns in the communion service!

Examining the range of our own Church tradition and considering the lost parts of our traditions can be hugely valuable in responding to new times and situations. Some parts of our tradition are no longer relevant to our calling today, but others can be the source of renewal for our Church in a new age. Of course, it is not always easy to tell which is which. Careful consideration of the tradition is important to equip ourselves to find our way about the tradition and learn how to study at least some traditions in depth so that these skills can be called on in the future.

Different interpretations

A key question of any study of Church tradition is how to interpret what we meet – whether that is in what was or is said, what was or is written, or what was or is currently done. Read, for example, the 39 Articles of the Church of England, the Doctrinal Clause of the 1932 Deed of Union of the Methodist Church or the Westminster Confession. After a time there is bound to be a phrase or sentence where you see that it could be interpreted in two or more ways and you may find yourself saying, 'Does it mean this or does it mean that?' Read some scholars on the subject and you still may not resolve your question. Rather you may find other possible interpretations that you did not think of originally. As with most studies in preparation for ministry courses, interpretation is unavoidable.

Handling different interpretations is a crucial part of our preparation. You need to be able to form your own views within the tradition to which you belong and at least to understand others. Practising the arguments and testing the evidence that supports the arguments should become a regular part of your engagement. Different interpretations sometimes mean one is right and others wrong. More often they show that the truth and its outworkings are complex and multifaceted.

You may in the process confirm, modify or radically change your original convictions. At the same time you may develop appropriate pride and face uncomfortable truth about your own tradition. Almost certainly you will finish your preparation aware that the Christian faith and the traditions which have expressed it over 2,000 years are richer and more diverse than you originally thought. If it strengthens your sense of being part of a wide river of living faith, it will have succeeded in helping you to understand and serve the Church better.

Going further

1.   Write down a list of six things you value from your own tradition.

2.   Write down six things you value in a tradition other than your own.

3.   Consider spending a few Sundays attending the church of a friend in a different denomination or Church tradition. Then have a meal with your friend to talk about the experience.

4.   Read a book about your own or another tradition.

Some suggestions are listed below.

Further reading

Gideon Goosen, *Bringing Churches Together: A Popular Introduction to Ecumenism*, World Council of Churches, 2002.

Angela Shier-Jones, *A Work in Progress. Methodists Doing Theology*, Epworth. 2005.

Stephen Sykes, *Unashamed Anglicanism*, Darton, Longman & Todd, 1995.

Barrie Tabraham, *The Making of Methodism*, Epworth Press, 1998.

Tony Tucker, *Reformed Ministry*, United Reformed Church, 2003.

B. G. Worrall, *The Making of the Modern Church*, SPCK, 1993.

10

Skills for ministry

There are often very different attitudes to learning skills for ministry. Here are two stories.

Mike came to me (Roger) to say that he had felt a call to preach and he wanted to become a local preacher. He had many of the gifts needed. He was a natural communicator, people liked him, and he had a real passion to tell people about Jesus, and could be very funny. I could see immediately that he might become a first-rate preacher. However, when I explained the training programme for preachers in the Methodist Church, he said he didn't think it was necessary. 'David didn't train to fight Goliath,' he said. 'He simply did what God called him to do. In fact, the armour and swords of the trained men were useless and only got in the way.' As a piece of theological reflection (see Chapter 12), I thought, it was interesting but flawed. Leaving aside whether the analogy between preaching and military combat is appropriate, there are a number of questions I posed. Did God call David to do this? Did David not learn the skills of using a sling as a shepherd boy and probably from his older brothers? Did not David learn to use a sword and armour as he went on as king to lead his armies against other adversaries? Thus with his gifts, he trained further so as to serve God and the people better. Despite all these (what I thought were) clever arguments, Mike took some convincing to take up the training programme. When he did eventually train he became a very skilled and able preacher.

Isobel, on the other hand, worked hard from the beginning. People had said to her from her teenage years that she ought to be a preacher. She had gained a lot from her minister, whom she admired greatly. She wanted to serve people as he had and so she practised hard, attended to all the feedback of her mentors and tried all the ideas that came from her studies. She was accepted as

> a local preacher because everyone saw how hard she had worked
> and because she could organize a service and speak passably
> but she was never inspiring and over the years, despite attending
> in-service and refresher days, she became a boring preacher.
> Although people liked her – she was a good listener and always
> remembered details about people's lives – they nevertheless
> stayed away from church when they heard she was taking the
> service. Indeed it was not until she has a personal crisis in her
> middle years that she recognized that this was not the area where
> her gifts lay. She trained as a Samaritan counsellor and was very
> effective in this work for the rest of her life. It was here, rather
> than as a preacher, that she saw a fulfilling of God's call on her life.

Now it is possible to draw a simple lesson from the combination of those two stories: namely, you need both a sense of call and a willingness to learn skills in order to minister. The call is needed to prompt you and sustain you. Skills are needed to carry out the calling effectively. Certainly that message is implicit, but there are other points that may be relevant for you as start to consider skills for ministry.

We bring a number of things to our preparation for ministry programmes and these influence how we engage in the programme. This is nowhere more evident than in learning the skills for ministry. What do we bring?

1. Ideas of ministry;

2. Established gifts and skills;

3. Attitudes to training.

Ideas of ministry

Isobel and Mike both brought ideas about the nature of the ministry, in this case the nature of the preaching ministry. Isobel had admiration for her own local minister and wanted to minister as he had. In other words, she saw the nature of preaching primarily through the work of one minister. For many people their concept of the nature of ministry is taken from the way it is expressed by someone they have known well and from whom they have received ministry – probably the local priest or minister. Even if they have not totally agreed with the person on everything and see the faults as well as gifts of the minister, the way the person has ministered provides an influential model of ministry. It may act as a default model at the back of the mind.

Mike also had a concept of ministry, though his was revealed in his biblical reference. He saw preaching, at least in part, as combative. His call to preach was a call to challenge evil, to proclaim the gospel whatever the cost and to win people for Christ. Again these ideas may have been drawn from people whom he admired. They certainly resonate with some important New Testament ideas. But perhaps this would make him less sympathetic to other concepts of preaching such as speaking to the pastoral situations of a congregation or gently kindling hope in an ageing and dispirited community.

These views of ministry that we carry are important. They may be key to how we have heard the call of God in the first place. We need to recognize, however, that the models of ministry that we bring will influence how we engage with training. We will probably value highly the aspects of training that appear to relate to or strengthen our view of ministry and have less time for things that don't quite fit. In other words, our 'pre-view' of ministry acts as a filter on what we notice and what we engage with.

In order for you to find the right place within the ministry of the Church and use the unique gifts that God has given us, you may have to develop your view of ministry. This does not mean rejecting the view that you bring with you, but it may mean being exposed to a wider range of ways of expressing the ministry, say by observing and working with a number of people. It may mean expanding your understanding of ministry, by reading what the Church has said about this ministry and calling and relating that to your own call.

Pause for thought

Who are the people who have influenced you?

What were the real strengths of their ministry?

How might their approach to ministry help and hinder your approach?

Established gifts and skills

On one level Mike had many of the gifts and skills he would need as a preacher. He was a good communicator, had a warm sense of humour and he had passionate faith. He also had a good working knowledge of the Bible and was used to leading group of people in a variety of church and work situations. Some of the skills, for example communication skills and leadership skills, he had developed in a work context where he had been a manager and then owned his own business. He could see, as I could, that these skills would transfer across into the new ministry. What he could not see was that this transfer would not be easy.

The transfer would not be straightforward, in part because the groups he would be working with were different. Voluntary gatherings in church are different from groups of employees who are paid to do what you ask them to as a manager and owner. You may have to inspire, to motive and to give people vision in both contexts, but in the latter there are other factors at work such as hanging on to one's job! It is interesting to note that transfer of skills from one context to another is difficult even for highly trained surgeons. Although many of the core skills for heart surgery, brain surgery and throat surgery appear to be the same, not many surgeons work in all three areas. The skills have to be combined with extensive knowledge of the focus and context.

Another reason why Mike's skills might not transfer easily is that the nature of the enterprise is radically different. Ultimately a preaching ministry is about making clear God's character and work and inviting people to respond to God's gracious invitation and call upon our lives. This is not the same as making a computer, repairing a car or selling apples. These activities make sense within an economic framework of exchange of goods and services. Preaching only makes sense within a Christian view of God and the world. The skills must be developed and used within that framework of understanding.

This links to another important reason why transfer of skills is not automatic. The development of skills in Christian ministry is not separate from the formation of character. If you are an airline pilot, passengers are rightly concerned that you have experience and skills to take off, fly and land a plane safely. Most travellers will be less bothered about whether you fiddle your taxes, are promiscuous or get drunk when off duty. If you are a minister these things matter. What you say, how you say it and how you live the rest of your life are all of a piece. Thus the development of skills needs to be related to a growing knowledge of God and of the Church, and the formation of your character.

Hence many people who expect their skills to transfer easily are surprised that they do not. Indeed some feel deskilled in the process of training and, if leaving full-time work or ceasing to use them in a familiar context, may lose confidence in their skills altogether for a time (there is more about this in Chapter 8).

The way to think about transferring your established skills is to think in terms of transplanting into another soil. When a plant is taken from one part of the world to another, there is no guarantee that the plant will flourish in its new environment. Nevertheless it is often very successful because careful attention is given in the early stages to ensure that the conditions are right for growth and help is offered by the gardener to make the transition. You will need to explore with others how your established skills relate to the new ministry, where they will fit in practice and where you need to make adjustments. You will need conversations too, in a variety of settings, about how your skills relate to the calling and life of the Church.

Pause for thought

What are the skills you have already that will be helpful in your new ministry?

How might those skills be differently used and understood in your new work?

Attitudes to training

Finally we can see in our stories two very different attitudes to training. Mike's attitude, at least at the beginning, was 'Training is unimportant. Calling is all. I don't need any training.' Isobel's was almost the opposite. Her view was 'Training is all-important: it will make me a preacher.' Both are clearly unhelpful attitudes to hold at the beginning of a preparation for ministry process. One will lead to non-engagement and may even foster arrogance – hardly an appropriate virtue for ministry. The other will tend to focus all the energy on techniques and miss out the wider framework of understanding God and self that is needed for mature ministry. Most people's attitude will be somewhere between the two, with a view that there are some skills to transfer, some to be developed and all within expanding views of the nature of ministry, the Church and God.

Pause for thought

Look at the list below. Under each area there are some examples of the skills (not an exhaustive list). Identify the skills you need for the ministry for which you are preparing. If the ministry for which you are preparing does not appear, add it and then use the skills lists to identify the skills you may need for your work.

Areas of skill

- **Leadership** – developing vision; ability to consult and collaborate; communication skills; ability to manage change; strategic thinking ability; listening to God, listening to people and listening to contexts; acting in appropriate ways in public for the Church.

- **Preaching** – exegetical skills; using commentaries; relating Bible exegesis and contemporary experience; sermon construction: finding and honing good illustrations, clear reading and speaking; ability to relate to a range of congregations and settings.

- **Leading worship** – ability to understand and construct appropriate liturgies; leading public prayers, meditations and liturgies; ability to use the arts and new technology in worship; skills in devising a variety of services, including all-age worship; an understanding of the theology and practice of baptism and the Eucharist.

- **Pastoral care** – listening skills; understanding of death, bereavement, mental illness; establishing and maintaining boundaries; confidentiality; relating theology and pastoral practice.

- **Administration** – good organization; time management skills; ability to write for different types of media; use filing systems; effective communication.

- **Group leadership** – knowledge of theories of groups and ability to use this knowledge; conflict management; ability to listen; good communication skills; ability to chair meetings; pastoral awareness; ability to read body language.

- **Outreach ministry** – awareness of contemporary culture; good interpersonal skills; ability to organize, to inspire and motive others; ability to articulate faith in ways that non-churched people can understand.

- **Youth work** – understanding of youth culture and models of youth work; ability to listen and relate to young people and their experiences; good interpersonal skills; ability to plan and run events, courses and programmes.

- **Pioneer ministries** – entrepreneurial gifts; a willingness to take risks; the ability to identify and win the confidence of different groups and cultures; the ability to form and lead new communities.

Developing ministerial skills

Clearly there are many different skills for different types of ministry. Some will be common to several ministries; others may be clearly connected to particular forms of ministry. There are some common processes to learning even quite diverse skills. Here are four.

Observation

On some courses students are told that they are to go on placement, but only to observe, at least in the first period. They are specifically prohibited from preaching, or visiting, or leading groups and meetings – even though they may have done some of these things before. Rather they are required to shadow someone else doing these things and observe closely without taking part. The practice of this is sometimes very frustrating for students who 'want to get on with it', but the rationale for this approach is not difficult to understand. Because 'doing' takes time, energy and effort one could get involved and easily miss important information and insight. Attention to the trees – pruning, repairing or cutting them down – may prevent you from seeing the wood – either the shape of the wood and its position on the hillside (macro) or the nature of the wood of which the trees are composed (micro). It may also stop you noticing the approach and techniques of an experienced lumberjack.

Not all courses or programmes will have this particular structure, but it is likely that disciplined observation will form some part of the way you develop ministerial skills. Even if it is not formally required, you may find yourself noticing things about the way those in ministry do things and the effect it has on others.

Observation can be enhanced by two practices. First, observing with some particular questions in mind may highlight aspects of the skill in context. What is the nature of the relationship between the minister and the people? How do the different aspects of this person's ministry work together? What is the context of this ministry and how does the context affect what happens? What model of ministry or mission operates in this setting? What image of God comes through in the work? These are questions that not only allow you to see aspects of ministerial skills but also to understand them in a particular location.

Second, careful description can open up real insight into the nature of ministerial skills. As part of your assessed work, you may have to write a report, offer a portfolio of observations and reflections, or give an oral presentation. This is often the most fruitful of exercises because it forces us to identify significant aspects of our observation and make them clear to others. Attempting to set down in an orderly form a description of what we have observed often highlights key points. Both these practices can be helped by the keeping of a journal (there is more information on journaling in Chapter 2).

The benefits of observation in developing ministerial skills are many. If you have come with some concept of the ministerial skills formed in your own church or circuit, it may alert you to other approaches. At the same time, it may allow you to see how skills are used in different contexts and perhaps what ideas of the Church and God lie behind certain actions. It will widen your knowledge base and give you more to draw on for the development of your own ministerial skills.

Of course, you may through observation see weaknesses and blind spots in the people you shadow. You may well pick up on how others see the minister and this may not be complimentary. Such information and opinion needs to be handled humbly, sensitively and generously. You are given a privileged position, especially if the observation is part of placement. Any reporting that is not confidentially handled could damage both trust and ministry. Likewise simply accepting and passing on other people's criticisms or gripes to other members of the local church or community may be destructive. If you have difficulties over things you observe, talk honestly with the minister and pose your observations as questions, trying all the time to understand and learn from the setting. Unless what you observe is criminal, in which case you would need to act according to proper procedures, you are simply observing another human being called into ministry and your learning is for your own development. Finally, remember that you have weaknesses and blind spots and these will be part of your ministry too. Guarding, supporting and encouraging each other's ministry are vital to building up the body of Christ. It is only when there is a bedrock of love and trust that people can speak painful truth and be heard (see Ephesians 4.15-16).

Action, reflection and feedback

Of course, a key part of the development of ministerial skills will be through practice. In most cases, skills will be practised and developed through a series of stepped stages designed to given familiarity and gradually build confidence. For example, a local preacher or lay Reader may well accompany an experienced person on a number of occasions to observe and take different roles in the act of worship – reading a lesson, leading prayers, offering a testimony or short reflection – before planning to preach a sermon. In our college context we have prepared people to take funeral services through a series of steps. The first step is observing priests conducting funerals on placement. This is followed later in the programme by a two-week course on aspects of death, dying and bereavement. One of the exercises on the course is to give students information about a 'deceased person' and ask them to prepare a short homily that they might preach at the funeral. They then preach this to a small group of peers while being videoed. They group watches the video with the person and they discuss how the preaching might be strengthened. In the period after the course, students are encouraged where appropriate in their placement to take responsibility for the preparation and conducting of a funeral service with the minister or priest alongside them for support. Of course, the real test comes when the person is in parish or circuit and has to prepare and lead a service on his or her own, but by this time the trainee ministers have usually developed enough confidence in their own skills to undertake the task.

In all the practice settings, two ways of gaining insight for further development are often used. The first is some form of reflection and *self-evaluation*. Asking questions such as, 'What do I feel went well? How did the other participants react at various points? Are there alternative ways of doing this? Where could I improve my skill?' Developing habits of self-evaluation can contribute towards positive development provided you keep the outcome in mind. This should not be about self-recrimination or negative introspection. Rather it should have the aim of improving and strengthening your ability.

The second is the use of *constructive feedback* from others. This may be formally arranged within the structure of the programme, where you may be observed by a tutor, supervisor, mentor or your peers. Alternatively it may be informally encouraged with the suggestion that you identify someone or a small group to work with you for this purpose. Either way the process should follow a simple pattern of identifying the strong points of what you did (affirmation), suggesting points to work on (identifying development) and offering suggestions as to ways of extending your ideas and actions or offering alternative ways of tackling something (constructive input). The balance of these elements is crucial. If the group simply praises everything you do, it may make you feel good but probably does little to help you. If the observers simply finds fault, you may lose confidence. If they do not offer ideas for you to try, you may not see how to go forward and equally feel dispirited. Some groups work on the 2 : 1:1 principle. That is, you find two things you want to affirm about a person's practice for every one weakness you identify; and for every one weakness, you offer a constructive suggestion. It is good to remember this when you help others, as well as when you are on the receiving end.

The two techniques – self-evaluation and constructive feedback – can inform each other and are often used in conjunction.

Apprenticeship and mentoring

At one time when people started a new job they were told to 'Go and sit beside Nellie, do what she does and learn the job from her.' After many years of debating how best people can learn skills, the ideas of apprenticeship and mentoring have made a major comeback. It is now common for mentoring arrangements to be made in many professional and semi-professional areas of work. Experienced practitioners not only know how 'to do it' but they have encountered lots of different and sometimes difficult situations and can draw on that wide experience when a new recruit meets problems.

Most preparation for ministry programmes will have a mentoring arrangement. Some will operate from the beginning, others for short periods, perhaps for an agreed period or connected with a placement. In other programmes the main mentoring will happen as you move from initial to continuing or practice phases of ministry. In some the mentor will be the supervisor (e.g., a training incumbent for curates), or it may be someone outside the immediate context of a placement or your work in ministry. In all cases the mentor acts as encourager, coach and conversation partner as you begin to do take the first steps of practising ministry.

The pattern of action, reflection and feedback will continue in the mentoring relationship, and this relationship also allows for deeper learning through concentrated work in one setting. This means the conversation can and should range over the contours of the context in which you work, the theology which informs your actions and your character and ministry. It should contribute to the fourth process, that of integration.

Integration

The ultimate aim of any preparation for ministry training programme is the integration of skills, theology and character. There is no one technique for achieving this and indeed it may be better seen as a lifelong process. There are nevertheless moments of integration which occur on the way. Some of the most satisfying moments of our own work have been on those occasion when someone preparing for ministry says, 'I have just realized how this fits together . . .' or 'I am making sense of this now . . .', and then goes on to tell us how they are integrating all that has been going on for them over the training time.

This is sometimes called 'reframing'. That is, finding a new frame through which to see all the elements that make up the picture. It is as if the old frame no longer works because the picture has been changed – you have added new ideas, skills and knowledge. A new frame is needed to hold all the elements in view in some kind of relationship and at the same time help you to appreciate all the elements in the right light. Choosing the right frame for a picture may take longer than choosing a picture (as I, Roger, found out recently when choosing a present for my wife), but when you get the right one it brings the pictures alive with meaning. Integration happens when we find a new frame.

Some of the impetus for integration will come from outside ourselves. Through the encounters with new situations of ministry and new theological ideas, the conversation with mentors or tutors, the feedback sessions and self-evaluations, there will be some external pressure on us to make sense of it all and combine the different elements together into a whole.

Some of the impetus will come from within us, quite naturally. Our minds are unsettled when things are out of harmony and there is an inner search for coherence in meaning that seems inbuilt. Psychologists call it 'cognitive dissonance', when our experiences and actions are out of line with our thinking. Our brains may in fact cause us to be disturbed until we have found some sort of resolution to the inner conflict and can make sense of it as whole. Therefore we can expect occasional unsettled periods in formation in general and as ministerial skills develop.

The two most important elements in achieving integration are the time and space for it to happen. Here quiet days and retreats, holidays and time off from study or ministry are as important as writing essays, journals and reports. In may happen halfway through training, or a year after you finish the preparation course. It is not unlike a fermentation process – once all the ingredients are in place the process has a timetable of its own that cannot be hurried. Integration will come when we are at the point for it and not before. We can help the process by cooperating. Deliberately posing questions for ourselves: 'How does this relate to that?' Or 'Do what I say I believe and what do I connect?' Or 'Are my skills growing at the same pace as my understanding of what I am doing?' All of these can help to stimulate the process, but it will work at its own pace.

Again a little like the fermentation process, a lot of energy is both used and released. The process of learning new skills is tiring enough, but seeking to integrate them into your commitment to God and the Church and develop your own identity can be occasionally exhausting. You may find that the work going on inside you takes its toll and you may need extra rest after a period of development and intense learning. On the other hand, integration moments can be very releasing of energy. As you see things in a new way you are energized for service and can work with renewed energy levels.

But perhaps the main point to have in mind is that integration is the goal towards which we are working. The relationship between integration and integrity counts, especially in ministry.

Going further

Go back through the Pause for thought sections in the chapter and list:

1.   The view of ministry you bring with you and what skills that view suggests.

2.   The skills you bring to preparation.

3.   The skills you need to develop.

Consider the four ways of growing into the skills identified above. What experience do you have of any or all of these?

Identify a moment of reframing in your life. What was the new way of seeing things you came to? What were the prompts and signs of it growing?

Further reading

Virginia Samuel Cetuk, *What to Expect in Seminary: Theological Education as Spiritual Formation*, Abingdon, 1998.

There are many books on the different skills for ministry. Here are two we have found particularly useful:

David Day, *A Preaching Workbook*, SPCK, 1998.

Paul Goodliff, *Care in a Confused Climate*, Darton, Longman & Todd, 1998 (on pastoral care).

Part Four: Understanding and caring for God's world

11

Mission and ministry

The Church is the only society which exists for the benefit of its non-members.

William Temple

Learning and changing through mission

When Jesus wanted his disciples to learn about mission, he gave them simple instructions and sent them out two by two with a particular task (Luke 9.1-6; 10.1-12). These periods of engaging in mission in the Gospels are followed by times of reflection with Jesus so that the lessons learned are retained for future ministry.

In the same way, all of us learn about mission best by being sent: gaining different experiences of God at work within and outside the Churches. This may take the form of a faith-sharing weekend with a team of others; helping on a soup run; doing door-to-door visiting while on a local church placement; visiting the local mosque; living in a flat on an inner city estate for a week or so; visiting a different country; spending time in a farming community; or becoming involved with the diocesan social responsibility group. For some in training, these experiences will be alongside what you may already be doing from day to day and from week to week: what may be different is the dimension of additional reflection. For others, the experiences of mission may involve being taken out of your normal routine and put into a new situation for a short time.

Whatever the experience may be, it is likely to be something which changes us deeply. Engaging in mission is transformational: we find that things change not just in the setting or the people we are working with but, profoundly, in ourselves. Reflection on those experiences both informally with our peers and formally with tutors and in writing reports is a vital part of the learning process. We gain a larger vision of the world and God's work within the world, and we carry the lessons forward for our own ministry and the life of the churches we will be called to serve.

However, it would be a mistake to think that mission is only about action, about doing. Mission is also a key area for thinking and reflection in the whole Church at the present time as we adjust to the immense changes taking place in our society. This chapter aims to give an overview of thinking about Christian mission in the Scriptures and the life of the Church and to highlight some of the live issues for the contemporary Church.

The God of mission and the mission of God

Christians believe in the God who has revealed himself in the Scriptures and, supremely, in Jesus Christ. This God is a God of deep and everlasting love for the whole of creation. God's love should not be understood as passive: standing back from the world and waiting. God's love is revealed in Scripture as active: searching and inviting and involved in the life of the world and the life of God's people. In all the major 'movements' of the Scriptures, in the life of Israel and in the life of the early Church, it is God who takes the initiative and God who becomes involved. God is a God of mission because he is first a God of active, searching, incomprehensible love.

Mission and the Old Testament

From the very beginning of the biblical story of this active, searching love, God invites and calls people to join in and to share this work of loving creation. The word mission comes from the Latin word for 'to send'. The Bible is the story of God calling and sending others to be messengers of his love and of his just and gracious rule. So Abram in Genesis 12 is called and sent. This sending is not simply for the sake of Abram and his immediate family but is for the sake of the whole world: 'in you all the families of the earth shall be blessed' (Genesis 12.3). Moses is called and sent by God to bring Israel out of Egypt to be God's own people. Throughout the Old Testament, Israel wrestles with the responsibilities of this calling. At its heart is the challenge to witness to God's grace and love not just in Israel but to the whole earth. This is the picture at the heart of the remarkable vision in Isaiah 2:

> In the days to come
>   the mountain of the Lord's house
> shall be established as the highest of the mountains,
>   and shall be raised above the hills;
> all the nations shall stream to it.
>   Many people shall come and say,
> 'Come, let us go up to the mountain of the Lord,
>   to the house of the God of Jacob;
> that he may teach us his ways
>   and that we may walk in his paths.'

> For out of Zion shall go forth instruction,
>   and the word of the Lord from Jerusalem.
> He shall judge between the nations,
>   and shall arbitrate for many peoples;
> they shall beat their swords into ploughshares,
>   and their spears into pruning-hooks;
> nation shall not lift up sword against nation,
>   neither shall they learn war any more. (Isaiah 2.2-4)

The goal of this mission in the Old Testament is establishing the reign or the rule or the kingdom of God. The fundamental marks of this kingdom are peace and freedom, justice and righteousness, through the whole earth. Many of the writings in the Prophets and the Psalms reflect on the tension between this vision of what life should be and what it has become. The Psalms proclaim in faith that God is king and reigns, often despite chaos, war and injustice: one day these will be set right (see Psalms 93–100). The prophets long for the day when this great reign of God will begin: their hopes focus more and more on the one who will come and establish that kingdom for ever. The kings of Israel and Judah have all in different ways fallen short of establishing peace and freedom, justice and righteousness. The one who will come, God's anointed messenger and king, will bring about this new kingdom:

> The spirit of the Lord God is upon me, because the Lord has anointed me; he has sent me to bring good news to the oppressed, to bind up the broken-hearted, to proclaim liberty to the captives, and release to the prisoners; to proclaim the year of the Lord's favour. (Isaiah 61.1-2)

A very important starting point for mission is to begin to 'mind the gap': to become aware in our own day of what the world is like (on the one hand) and what the world is called to be (on the other). Much of the groundwork for this

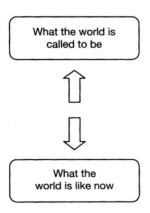

vision of what the world is called to be is to be found in the study of the Old Testament where the themes and range of the material are concerned with the whole of human life. The themes of the New Testament give greater weight and focus to the life of the emerging Christian communities and their concerns. This is one of the reasons why giving due priority to Old Testament study is a vital part of preparation for ministry. It is impossible to go to one or two key texts in the Old Testament to find a blueprint for God's call for human society. The whole must be read and studied and reflected upon in dialogue with the life of the world and vision for mission and change.

Jesus and the first disciples

This Old Testament background is also essential to enable us to understand the mission of Jesus, God's Son, who is sent to proclaim and to establish the kingdom of God in fulfilment of this great Old Testament hope. The message of Jesus must not be reduced to a gospel of individual salvation through the forgiveness of sins. The message of Jesus has at its very heart this hope, this new vision for the world, which is summed up in the shorthand phrase 'the kingdom of God':

> Now after John was arrested, Jesus came to Galilee, proclaiming the good news of God, and saying, 'The time is fulfilled, and the kingdom of God has come near; repent, and believe in the good news.' (Mark 1.14-15)

Jesus' ministry includes both teaching about the kingdom and signs of the kingdom's presence through miracles of healing and deliverance. In Luke's Gospel, Jesus' public ministry begins in the synagogue in Nazareth as he reads aloud (and applies to himself) the manifesto of Isaiah 61 (Luke 4.16-21). Following the pattern of the Old Testament, from the very beginning of his ministry, Jesus calls others to be involved in the mission of establishing and proclaiming God's reign:

> He went up the mountain and called to him those whom he wanted, and they came to him. And he appointed twelve, whom he also named apostles, to be with him, *and to be sent out* to proclaim the message. (Mark 3.13-14)

The mission of the disciples is to live and to proclaim the message of the kingdom. The mission of Jesus himself is, of course, far greater than this. Jesus not only lives and proclaims the kingdom of God. It is through Jesus' death on the cross and the power of the resurrection that the kingdom is established:

> For in him all the fullness of God was pleased to dwell, and through him God was pleased to reconcile to himself all things, whether on earth or in heaven, by making peace through the blood of his cross. (Colossians 1.19-20)

> But now in Christ Jesus you who were once far off have been brought
> near by the blood of Christ. For he is our peace; in his flesh he has made
> both groups into one and has broken down the dividing wall, that is, the
> hostility between us. He has abolished the law with its commandments
> and ordinances, so that he might create in himself one new humanity in
> place of the two, thus making peace, and might reconcile both groups to
> God in one body through the cross, thus putting to death that hostility
> through it. So he came and proclaimed peace to you who were far off and
> peace to those who were near. (Ephesians 2.13-17)

For this reason, at the heart of the gospel message which the Church proclaims
and at the heart of mission is the story of the death and resurrection of Jesus
Christ (see also 1 Corinthians 15.1-3). It is only by his death and resurrection that
the kingdom is established and the possibilities of reconciliation and renewal for
all people and all creation are held open. The gap between God's vision for
creation and the reality is very wide. The only possibility for a new beginning and
the redeeming of creation is through an event as deep and radical as the
crucifixion and resurrection of God's Son out of love for the world.

In every time and in every place the Church is called to demonstrate, live and
proclaim this good news: a truth emphasized by the different passages in the
New Testament where the early disciples are commissioned by Christ:

> Thus it is written, that the Messiah is to suffer and to rise from the dead
> on the third day, and that repentance and forgiveness of sins is to be
> proclaimed in his name to all nations, beginning from Jerusalem. You are
> witnesses of these things. And see, I am sending upon you what my Father
> promised; so stay in the city until you have been clothed with power from
> on high. (Luke 24.46-49)

The Spirit and mission

Mission is at the heart of God's grace and love: the Father sends the Son. The
Father and the Son together send the Holy Spirit. Part of the work of the Spirit
(and a particular emphasis in Luke's theology) is to empower the Church in this
task of mission:

> But you will receive power when the Holy Spirit has come upon you; and
> you will be my witnesses in Jerusalem, in all Judea and Samaria, and to the
> ends of the earth. (Acts 1.8)

This empowering of the Spirit is worked out in all kinds of ways in the accounts
of Jesus' ministry in the Gospels and in the story of the early Church in the book

of Acts. Part of the study in reflection on mission is reflection on the ways in which the Holy Spirit is and can be empowering the Church today in a whole variety of ways to demonstrate and articulate good news.

Check it out

Follow through these references to the Spirit and mission in the book of Acts.

- Acts 1.4-5   The promise of the Spirit
- Acts 2.1-21   Pentecost
- Acts 4.31   A new filling of the Spirit
- Acts 8.14-16   The Spirit and the Samaritans
- Acts 10.44-48   The Spirit and the Cornelius
- Acts 13.1-3   The Spirit and the church in Antioch
- Acts 16.6-10   The Spirit guides the mission
- Acts 19.1-7   The Spirit and the Ephesians

Models of Christian mission

The understanding of Christian mission has been worked out in different ways in different generations in the life of the Church. Part of the study of mission is understanding these differences and the evolving story. One of the dynamics in the story is the changing cultural context in which the Church finds itself in different places and in different generations.

In the first three hundred years or so of its life the Church was a minority faith in an indifferent and at times hostile culture. To become a Christian was a major and counter-cultural step for both Jews (who would be alienated from their own communities) and for Gentiles (who would be stepping outside the normal social customs of their day and who might attract economic or social hardship or physical persecution). Every community of Christians in every kind of setting knew itself to be in a missionary context. For the first hundred years or so of its life the Church had very few permanent buildings. It could not rely on any support from the society in which it found itself in terms of state support or approval: from time to time the opposite was the case. It was subject to frequent misrepresentation and misunderstanding by the equivalent of the media of the day.

Among the structures for mission and Church life which emerged in that context were:

- An emphasis on deliberate and intentional Christian community, meeting together regularly for worship, nurture, teaching and fellowship;

- An emphasis on the Christian community being different from the society around it in terms of its moral codes, its culture, its allegiance to the state, its attitude to wealth;

- A pattern of lengthy preparation for adult baptism (known as the catechumenate) which was thorough and intensive over a period of two to three years and followed by a lifelong call to intentional discipleship;

- Structures for pastoral ministry and mutual care exercised by the whole body of Christ which depended on a small number of stipendiary ministers but which were effective in sustaining and enabling the whole Church.

With the conversion of the Roman Emperor Constantine in AD 313, Christianity moved from being a minority and sometimes persecuted counter-cultural faith to the official religion of the Roman Empire. This was, over time, a momentous change. The Church now had permanent and (sometimes) lavishly endowed buildings. In various ways, the wider culture was gradually less resistant and then more positively supportive of Christian faith and worship. More and more people were baptized as infants. The Christian faith became the normal way to live within the society of the late Empire.

This was a very different missionary situation. There was a loss of the distinctive emphasis on Christians meeting together to develop and preserve a distinctive community and identity. The lengthy process of teaching prior to adult baptism disappeared: children learned the faith now as they were growing up. Christian teaching was woven into the fabric of the year and cycle of the seasons. Structures of ministry became increasingly professionalized: a larger number of full-time and paid ministers serving, increasingly, the majority of the population. The Church developed new structures as a way of recognizing its responsibilities to minister to and serve the whole of society as opposed to a small group within that society.

The whole Church did not move in the whole of its life to this new way of understanding itself. The older forms and ways of mission were still necessary beyond the boundaries of the Roman Empire as missionaries sought to take the gospel beyond what we now call Christendom. Within areas which were nominally Christian there were movements for renewal and more intentional discipleship, the most remarkable and long-lasting of which was the monastic movement.

Broadly speaking, these two ways of being Church and seeing mission continue to coexist throughout Christian history. At the Reformation in England, the newly established Church of England continued to frame its identity around a 'Christendom' model. Its aim was to serve a society in which everyone was assumed to be a member of the national Church unless they specifically opted out. By contrast, the Methodist Church from its foundation was much more of a self-consciously missionary movement seeking to call to a living faith those who in reality knew very little about Christianity. Early Methodism took on therefore some of the key characteristics of the early Church in its mission (fostering communities of faith, careful teaching of adult disciples). As Methodism became more established and recognized within the United Kingdom, it took on more of the characteristics of a 'Christendom' Church. Over the same period, the Church of England slowly began to learn lessons about what it means to be a Church in mission in its own culture from the Methodist Church, from other Churches, and from the expansion of Christianity throughout the world through the missionary movement.

Mission in the present day

Over the last 25 to 30 years – and particularly since 1990 – mission has become progressively more central in the thinking of both Churches. The Church of England has gradually adopted a self-consciously missional identity in relation to its own society and culture, probably for the first time since its inception. The Methodist Church has, in a similar movement, been recalled to its roots as a movement of mission. Undoubtedly, both of the Churches have been led to examine their own identity by the rapid decline in church attendance and membership over the last generation. This self-examination has drawn on the renewal of a theology of mission in the world-wide Church to nurture a strong sense of the Church as a missionary community called to share in God's mission to the world and to embody God's love in the whole of human society.

The five marks of mission

There is no single, neat and all-encompassing way of summing up what is meant by mission in the life of the Church. No single Bible verse or definition can do it justice. However, in 1988, the worldwide Lambeth Conference of the Bishops of the Anglican Communion approved the following statement of the 'five marks of mission'. The five marks have become generally accepted as a helpful summary within the Church of England and the wider Anglican community:

- To proclaim the good news of the kingdom;

- To teach, nurture and baptize new believers;

- To respond to human need with loving service;

- To seek to transform unjust structures of society;

- To strive to safeguard the integrity of creation and sustain and renew the earth.

The first mark should be seen as an overarching heading: to proclaim the good news of the kingdom, as Jesus did, should include each of the other elements. The second mark sets the fulfilling of the great commission of Matthew 28.19-20 (to teach, nurture and baptize new believers – what we normally call evangelism) within the overall context of mission: as part of the whole, and first in order of precedence, but not the whole of what the Church means by mission. The third mark emphasizes loving service to human need: living out the parable of the Good Samaritan in the lives of individual Christians, the life of congregations and the life of the wider Church. The fourth emphasizes the importance of not simply addressing symptoms but causes as we seek together to establish the kingdom of God. This will mean the Churches, recognized ministers and denominations being willing to name injustice and to work for the transformation of structures. The fifth mark (added after the first four) reflects the truth that God's love is not simply for humankind and human society but for the whole of creation. Taken together, the five marks provide a good and helpful summary of Christian mission for a minister or congregation.

The Methodist Church in the United Kingdom has developed a number of key documents in recent years which stress the importance of mission including the text *Our Calling*, which offers a pattern for the development of each local congregation. In 2004, the Methodist Conference adopted a statement of Priorities for the Methodist Church which sets mission at the heart of the Churches' calling:

> In partnership with others wherever possible, the Methodist Church will concentrate its prayers, resources, imagination and commitments on this priority:

> To proclaim and affirm its conviction of God's love in Christ, for us and for the entire world; and renew confidence in God's presence and action in the world and in the Church.

> As a way towards realising this priority, the Methodist Church will give particular attention to the following:

>> Underpinning everything we do with God-centred worship and prayer

>> Supporting community development and action for justice, especially among the most deprived and poor – in Britain and worldwide

>> Developing confidence in evangelism and in the capacity to speak of God and faith in ways that make sense to all involved

Encouraging fresh ways of being Church

Nurturing a culture in the Church which is people centred and flexible.[1]

Contemporary issues in mission

There is more than one way of seeing any complex subject. In one of the best and most concise introductions to Christian mission, J. Andrew Kirk identified in 1999 six issues in worldwide Christian mission which are particular challenges and need attention in the present day. They form an interesting contrast to the five marks: there is some overlap but also significant differences.

The gospel in the midst of cultures

The Christian gospel is conveyed through human culture. The early Church had to address cultural questions from the very beginning (see Acts 15 for the classic passage). The Church in the present day needs to decide how it will relate to a multiplicity of cultures as society experiences a process of rapid and global change. Which aspects of Church life are essential to the Christian gospel? Which aspects of Church life can be left behind as the Church is established in a new context? In one of the modern classics on mission, *Christianity Rediscovered*, the North American Roman Catholic priest Vincent Donovan describes his wrestling with these issues in his mission to the Masai peoples of Central Africa. To reach the Masai effectively, Donovan realizes, he must abandon much of his own cultural inheritance of Church life and see the gospel give new shapes and forms to the Church in a new context. The Church in the West has been slow to learn these lessons as we seek to reach out cross-culturally across the generations and across social or racial divisions. The recent Church of England report, *Mission-shaped Church*, accepts the need to find fresh expressions of Church life if we are to be effective in taking the gospel beyond the fringe of our present congregations.

Justice for the poor

If we read the Bible seriously, we cannot help but notice a concern for justice for the poor in both the Old and the New Testament. When we set that beside the massive problems of global poverty and debt in the developing nations we see perhaps the greatest gap of all between the ideals of the kingdom of God and the reality of the world around us. Wrestling with the Churches' response to this situation takes preparation for ministry into the study of poverty and debt in our own society and globally. It will mean exploring the Churches' role in securing justice for the poor:

both in terms of direct giving and sponsoring aid programmes on the one hand and working for lasting change through movements such as Make Poverty History. It will mean taking seriously schemes such as diocesan and district links to different areas of the world – becoming involved and committed to change the situation.

Encounter with the religions of the world

Most Christians in Britain will now be conscious that we live in a multi-faith society. In some of our major cities there are now more active adherents of other world faiths than there are regular attenders at the churches. In most major towns and cities there will be a public centre of worship for one or other of the major religious communities. Since the attacks on the World Trade Center in September, 2001, the importance of building dialogue between different religious communities has been apparent to Christians of all persuasions. Preparing for recognized Christian ministry means taking this dialogue seriously and thinking through its different dimensions: both a Christian view of other faiths and of inter-faith dialogue, and learning something at least about the major world faiths which you are likely to encounter in public ministry.

Overcoming violence and building peace

In the Old Testament tradition, peace is seen as one of the goals and marks of the kingdom of God. In the New Testament, Jesus singles out the peace makers in the seventh Beatitude (Matthew 5.9). How are the Christian citizen, the Christian Church and the Christian minister to act and to speak in the context of increasing violence both within the United Kingdom and worldwide? In the last generation, Christians have played a significant role in seeking reconciliation and lasting peace in Northern Ireland and in South Africa (though we also need to remember that the Christian faith contributed to the conflict in both situations). Part of Christian mission is pondering the appropriate response of the Churches to, for example, gun crime in the inner cities (where Christians have joined with others in taking civil action); and to the recent invasion of Iraq (where the Churches were unanimous in their opposition to the military action). Seeking peace in society demands, of course, that the Church seeks peace also in its own life, resolving differences honestly and courteously wherever possible. There is a mission perspective on the acrimonious public debates that have marked the life of the Churches in recent years.

Care of the environment

The Christian faith proclaims a God who is creator of heaven and earth and declares that humanity is in a particular relationship of responsible stewardship of the natural environment. Again, there is a manifest gap between this ideal and the exploitation of the earth's resources by the world's richest nations. This gap is now affecting not only the economies of the poorer nations (through, for example, deforestation and the changing of the natural environment) but the very climate of the earth. Responsible stewardship as part of the Churches' mission therefore embraces sensible approaches to recycling of waste and the consumption of resources, through the raising of awareness to, once again, political campaigning and action. All of these issues and others are the practical outworking of the love of God for the world and the seeking of justice both in our own generation and for the sake of generations still to come.

Evangelism and Christian nurture

As part of the shift towards being a Church which is self-consciously missionary in relation to its own culture, the Church in the United Kingdom has been attempting to learn lessons about effective evangelism and nurture in a context where people outside the Churches know less and less about Christian faith. The general movement here has been from a concept of evangelism based on 'crisis' to one which shows a greater awareness of a process or journey of faith, albeit one punctuated by one or more crisis moments. When Billy Graham (or other evangelists) preached and invited people to make a response of faith from the 1950s to the 1980s they were largely preaching to people who had learned the Christian story as children. An invitation to respond in faith was a way of inviting people to see this story in a different way and to recognize its implications for their lives. After a conversion in this context, being nurtured in faith was simply a case of being reminded of truths people had learned long ago. Joining a church was a case of going back to a community and pattern of life and worship which had meant something at an earlier stage in life.

Increasingly, the generations growing up after World War II never learned the story and had never been part of the life of the Churches. Evangelism cannot therefore simply be based on an appeal to something which has been learned but never understood. The faith needs to be taught from first principles and over time. John Finney's key research, *Finding Faith Today*, published in 1992, has led to a reworking of the strategy of the Churches in evangelism around the theme of journey and gradual conversion. Churches which have grasped the lessons of the research have therefore changed their mode of evangelism to the offering of a course of ten or fifteen weeks as an introduction to Christian faith. In a similar way, there has been an increased emphasis on a process of intentionally forming disciples in the years immediately following conversion and baptism and, again, a range of materials is available to help Churches respond to this need. In very recent years, there has been a renewed awareness of a growing spiritual search in our wider society and the need for the Churches to listen to this experience and develop appropriate ways of addressing it.

Finally, it is being increasingly recognized that for a newly converted adult Christian to join a church is less and less straightforward. The person may themselves be coming from a very different social and cultural background. While it is one thing to feel at home in the halfway house of an Emmaus or Alpha course, it is quite another to start to attend the main Sunday morning service. For that reason, the attention of the Churches is shifting more and more in the present decade to developing new forms of Church life around those who are finding faith from different backgrounds.

God's mission

Like every area of formation, understanding and caring about God's world is not a detached academic exercise. In this, as in every other way, we learn through different experiences in life and in training, we learn through dialogue with fellow students, we learn through practical service. Our learning can challenge our own character and lifestyle in profound ways. The different areas of reflection connect together: as we come to a deeper appreciation of God's grace and love, so we grasp (and are grasped by) a deeper desire to share in God's mission to the world.

Going further

1.   What for you is the most important aspect of mission in the life of the Church and why?

2.   Give some examples from your own story of the way a situation has been transformed by the love and commitment of Christians. Give examples of ways in which you have been changed by engaging in mission.

Further reading

Graham Cray (ed.), *Mission-shaped Church: Church Planting and Fresh Expressions of Church in a Changing Context*, Church House Publishing, 2004.

Vincent Donovan, *Christianity Rediscovered*, second edition, SCM Press, 2001.

John Finney, *Finding Faith Today*, Bible Society, 1992.

J. Andrew Kirk, *What is Mission? Theological Explorations*, Darton, Longman & Todd, 1999.

Ann Morisey, *Beyond the Good Samaritan: Community Ministry and Mission,* Mowbray, 1997.

For details of fresh expressions of church in the Church of England and the Methodist Church see www.freshexpressions.org.uk

For more advanced students:

David Bosch, *Transforming Mission: Paradigm Shifts in the Theology of Mission,* Orbis Books, 1991.

12

Theological reflection

If you have made it this far in the book, you realize that preparation for ministry will add a few new words to your vocabulary! Words such as vocation, liturgy, formation and theology may not have been part of your daily conversation up to now, but they crop up frequently in ministry training.

This does not just apply to training for ministry.

My father (writes Roger) said to me as an 'eager to help' ten-year-old, 'Bring me a hammer from the shed.' I went to the shed to collect a hammer, only to find that there were six or more different types of hammer. They ranged from a small metal-headed hammer, through wooden mallets and heavy claw hammers, to two sizes of sledge hammer, one of which I could not lift. I realized now that I was missing some vital pieces of information. I didn't know the names of the different hammers and I was not really clear which hammer was best suited to the particular job. Had I known this information, it would have saved two or three trips from the house to the shed to provide the right one. As I ventured into the world of DIY I needed to extend my vocabulary in order to learn and do more.

In this book, we have introduced in each chapter some of the words that are needed to prepare for ministry for precisely this same reason, so that you can become familiar with the words and their use and so that you have a reference point to use as you prepare for your future work.

So far, so good. But now comes the phrase 'theological reflection'. Theological reflection is a phrase you are almost bound to hear in the context of preparation for ministry. What on earth does it mean, and what has it got to do with ministry? The purpose of this chapter is to explore this idea and see how it fits into your programme. Before that let me share two stories.

Jenny and Markus meet up with some of their friends for a drink and a meal. The conversation turns to the recent natural disaster, which has badly affected the lives of thousands of people, many of whom have died. Knowing that the couple are Christians, one of the friends asks, 'Why should God allow this to happen?' This is no easy question, but both try to give an answer. Markus says that God has made the world in such a way that chance and choice are important. Only by making a world that evolves can love and freedom really exist. If God constantly intervened to stop things going wrong, we would be no more than human robots. Jenny says that although she doesn't know why people suffer, she believes that God shares in the pain. She mentions her sister who is currently going through chemotherapy and is not guaranteed to survive, but who feels God is very close to her. Jenny says that Jesus' dying on the cross is a message about God sharing in our pain. God also prompts us to good in the face of tragedy, as can be seen in the number of people who have volunteered to help those in need and the money given for relief.

Jo gets into a bit of argument with a workmate. The subject is a newspaper report saying that a prisoner who killed a child when he himself was a young teenager is about to be released from prison and given anonymity to begin a new life, having served nine years in youth prison. The mother of the murdered child is quoted as saying she thinks it is a disgrace, that she can never have her child back, and the murderer should spend the rest of his life in prison. Jo tries to defend the idea of forgiveness and a new start. His mate says he is a soft-hearted Christian and this action denies the victim justice. Jo says that Jesus forgave even those who put him to death and asks us to forgive, to break the cycle of hurt and pain. Of course, one needs to see that people are truly sorry for what they have done and not going to be a danger to others but then there should be the possibility of a new start. While he didn't think he convinced his mate, Jo thought that at least he had tried to share his beliefs. A couple of weeks later he bumps into someone he hasn't met for years. The last time they met was when this person did something that resulted in Jo losing his job. There is an uncomfortable conversation, and Jo is surprised at how angry he stills feels towards this person. Later he wonders what his attitude should

> be towards this old acquaintance, especially in view of his recent
> argument about forgiveness.

Although Jo, Markus and Jenny might not use the word, they were all involved in
theology. The basic meaning of the word theology is 'God-talk' or 'God-thought'.
As they talked with their friends or colleague each was trying to express their
belief in God in relation to everyday life and its questions. In Jo's case it went a bit
further. His theological conversation – what he said he believed – came back to
him and caused him to think again about his own attitudes and actions. You might
say that his reflection on meeting his old 'friend' was theological, in that he posed
for himself the question: 'How can I be consistent about what I believe both in
what I say and what I do?'

Like the word *theology*, the notion of *theological reflection* is rooted in ordinary
attempts to make sense of our faith, our world and our lives. All of us are already
familiar with it – we do it already. It is part of how we make sense of life as
Christians. So in preparation for ministry, attention to theological reflection is a
continuation of what we have being doing before. However, it now takes on a
new significance. As ministers in the Church we not only have to make sense of
our individual actions and beliefs but also the actions of the Church and our
actions as public representatives of the Church (and sometimes, in a way, of
God). In training, we need to think further about the meaning of theological
reflection and how to do it in order to ensure that our ministry and the mission
of the Church conveys what we believe about God.

Theological reflection is . . .

Broadly speaking theological reflection can be seen as a perspective, a skill (or
set of skills) or a process. Examining each may help us understand better what
the term means and how we might engage with it in the process of preparing
for ministry.

A perspective

A perspective is a way of looking at something from a particular viewing point or
interest. Any one event can be looked from different perspectives. A change in
government policy on education, for example, could be viewed from an
economic and from a political perspective. In each viewing different aspects or
dimensions of the subject will be highlighted. The same initiative could also be
viewed from a legal, psychological or moral perspective. Theological reflection
sometimes means taking a theological perspective on an object or an event. In

other words, seeing something through theological eyes, identifying and discussing dimensions that are to do with God and God's purposes. As the slogan goes, 'What is the God angle on this?'

In one sense that is exactly what the Old Testament prophets did. They looked at the unfolding events of social and political history through the lens of God's intention and purpose. They picked out, highlighted and drew attention to the theological meaning of what was happening around them. Christians by definition have a theological world view. We view the world in a certain way, believing that it is created by a loving God, who has purpose for the creation and is involved in its ongoing life through the Holy Spirit, who has been revealed by Jesus Christ and who acted in Christ to redeem and renew the world and will bring all things into God's purpose at the end. To take this view and to seek to live by it, in faith, is to have a theological perspective on the world. Every time you pray, or you talk about your faith, or you try to live in a way that reflects what you believe as a Christian, you are acting theologically. It means too that you take a theological perspective into every situation. Every issue, question or event can be looked at from this theological point of view.

Theological reflection then is a way of looking at the world with which you will be familiar already. It is name for something you already know and, like the man who discovers that he has been speaking prose all his life, you may wonder what the fuss is about. The answer to that is that although we may take a theological view of the world there are often major blind spots and flaws where we fail to make the connection between our faith and the world around us. While we may be familiar with it already we can and often need to develop our capacity for theological reflection, especially if we are to minister and lead others in their discipleship. This leads us to the second way of conceiving of theological reflection.

A skill

One of the aims of the preparation for ministry programme will almost certainly be to develop further your skills of theological reflection. Notice the phrasing I have used here. It is to *develop further* your skill, not to learn it from scratch. As we suggested above, Christian commitment is a way of seeing the world, a world view. This means that each of us on the Christian faith journey will be trying, however successfully or unsuccessfully, to live our lives based on this view. As a Christian you will have already tried to work out your attitude to a number of issues and situations or perhaps developed your understanding of God through some particular experience. You may have worked through this by talking with others, by reading the Bible or books by other people of faith, listening to sermons and talks, by asking, 'What would Jesus have done?' or 'What should I as a Christian do here?' No doubt your thinking will have also happened in a less formal, more intuitive way by sensing what was the Christian thing to do or Christian attitude to hold. Extending, examining and informing this process, already at work within you, is the intention in theological education.

Broadly speaking there are three ways of nurturing theological reflection as a skill:

1.   Through practice in a variety of contexts;

2.   Through becoming self-conscious and critical of one's own approach;

3.   Through broadening the knowledge base of Scripture and tradition.

Practice in a variety of contexts

It has been suggested that the heart of theological reflection is a conversation – a conversation between experience and the theological tradition. This is a helpful way of seeing things because conversation has a number of aspects.

First, good conversation is open. It may simply be an exchange of anecdotes, information and views which leaves the conversation partners the same, but there is always a possibility that one or both partners in a conversation may be changed by the dialogue, a new thought provoked, a new attitude considered, or a different view of some familiar experiences taken on board. Sometimes, in the discussion there may be a creative moment which results in all the participants in the conversation breaking through to new insight together that none was capable of alone.

Second, you can get better at conversation. The way to get better at conversation is, of course, to engage in more conversations. Programmes of preparation for ministry will push you into having conversations of various types in order to develop your skills at theological reflection.

Some of these conversations will be with others on your course, who, inevitably, will be different in experience and conviction from yourself and there will be much to be gained from a genuine dialogue with them. It will give you practice in articulating your theological views and insights and considering other ways of seeing and approaching things. When a group task is required and there is a need to come to a common mind on something, practice is offered at finding creative ways through disagreement.

Other conversations will also be with tutors or teachers, mentors or experienced practitioners, where there may be deliberate prompting questions posed for you. 'Where did you see God in the situation?' 'What are the key points of this biblical passage that you would want to communicate in a sermon, and how might they apply to the congregation?' 'What view of the Church and ministry did you observe on placement?' 'What biblical image might you choose to describe your personal development over this last year?' These are all questions that might be posed for conversation. In most cases, they have no right answer. Rather they are opportunities to practise thinking by talking aloud from a theological perspective. Such theological conversations could focus on almost anything – reflecting on your paid employment, or on popular culture such as films and books, or on news events and topical ethical dilemmas, as well as Church practices or views of the atonement.

You may have realized by now that even where the conversation is with a fellow student or a tutor there is another kind of conversation going on at the same time. The conversation is between yourself and the theological tradition that is already inside you. You are having a conversation with yourself and reassessing your own views, perhaps to strengthen them, to modify them or to change them.

Writing essays is another form of conversation. When you are reading the thoughts of others, trying to understanding and evaluate them and get your own thoughts into order, then trying to express these on paper, again you are having a form of conversation within yourself and developing your thought processes for theological reflection. The reason why essay writing remains a key part of most training, and why people often find it very taxing to complete a piece of writing, is precisely because it causes a person to think deeply and work at theological conversation. The process can have significant and lasting effects on the way we think about and approach issues other than the one which we addressed in the assignment.

Becoming self-conscious and critical of one's own approach

People who take the advanced driving test are asked to do an odd thing. For a part of the test they are asked to speak aloud what they are doing as they are driving. The commentary may be, 'I am thinking about turning right at the next junction, so I am now looking in my rear view mirror to see what is behind me, I am signalling and slowing down slightly by using my foot brake . . .' At first sight it seems strange to be saying these things out loud for someone who is already a driver but the reason for it is both sensible and potentially very effective for making better drivers. When we first start to learn to drive, of course, we are very conscious of what we are doing because much of it is new and difficult. When we have learned to drive and passed the test we become less conscious of the individual parts that make up driving competence. These become subconscious and integrated into the way we drive. This is natural and helpful but it has a flaw. The fact that it goes into our subconscious means it is difficult to change and any faults in our driving are deeply embedded. Our partner or a friend may say to us that we leave braking late but it probably will have no effect on our general driving because the way we drive has become part of our habit of driving. The designers of the advanced driving test have recognized that if you want a person to develop better driving skills you need to bring to the surface the way that person drives, so that their habits can be recognized and, if necessary, changed. By doing this you can help the driver to become more self-conscious of their faults, so as to be able to correct them. It not only addresses aspects of driving that can be improved, it also gives the person on the ADT a way of examining their own practice to improve it on future occasions.

This approach of helping people become self-conscious of their way of doing something has become widespread. Following the writing of Donald Schön, it has become common to talk about the 'reflective practitioners',[1] meaning people who reflect on their way of thinking and doing things so as to develop better practice. It applies in all sorts of spheres of life from managers to nightclub bouncers and has much relevance for those in public ministry within and for the Church.

Everyone develops ways of thinking and approaching new situations and after a time, as in driving, these slip below the surface and 'work automatically'. The way we think about God, the way we use the Bible and the way we decide what to do in certain difficult situations can all fall into this category. In thoughtful programmes of preparation for ministry attention is given not only to engaging in conversation to develop one's skills of theological reflection but also to helping people examine the ways they have learned to think and approach issues. This is often achieved by offering some methods or processes for theological reflection (see below) against which to identify and test your own approach. It may also be helpful to understand one's own personality type and preferred way of learning (see Chapter 13). Most important is the increasing self-awareness that accompanies the process of learning and allows us to make changes in the way we think and approach issues. Together with the extended conversations, this enables us to be more skilled in our theological reflecting.

Broadening the knowledge base of Scripture and tradition

A third way in which theological reflection skills can develop during training is by learning more about the Bible and the tradition. As the breadth of your knowledge increases there is literally more material to draw on for looking at and exploring the world around in theological terms. You will know more about the Bible and ways of reading it, more about the history and mission of the Church and where it has been 'successful' and where it has 'failed', more about the ways people have thought about, preached about and prayed to God. In the conversations you have there will be more to bring into play, and in terms of self-awareness you may see some of the difficulty as well as strength of your particular ways of thinking by seeing how others have thought through Christian faith. You will be encouraged not only to learn and understand these things but also to evaluate them and be critical of them – not in order to be negative or destructive, but so as to build up your own Christian convictions in a robust and healthy way and to be able to present and defend beliefs. You will also be encouraged to apply your new learning to current situations and issues and this too is part of developing the skills of theological reflection.

A word of warning, however. Because some courses of study are divided into separate disciplines sometimes people do not transfer their critical thinking from one part of the curriculum to another. It is possible to write a high-quality piece of work on some aspect of Paul's first letter to the Corinthians in the New Testament module, and then when using 1 Corinthians in practical theology as part of discussion of how to respond to some contemporary issues, to forget all the critical discussion that was explored in the New Testament class and revert to using the Scripture as a kind of prooftext. This is not a phenomenon confined to theology, it is widespread in much formal study. It is important to remember that as your base of knowledge broadens you need to self-consciously carry that into other areas of study and ultimately into the whole of your life and work.

In all these ways theological reflection can be seen as a skill to nurture and develop and as we suggested at the beginning of this section, the more the skills you develop, the more able you are to inhabit a theological world view and live in and from it.

A process

For shorthand you might say that theological reflection is a process 'to make sense of experience in the light of the gospel'.

The origins of the idea are sometimes traced to Joseph Cardijn, a Roman Catholic priest in Belgium in the early part of the twentieth century. Cardijn was concerned for the plight of workers and, at his father's deathbed, dedicated himself to the cause of workers. In 1912 he began organizing a young working women's club. The group of women was divided into cells according to place of work, and Cardijn challenged each cell to Christianize its place of work. These cells took the form of study circles in which all had a participating role and each relied on each other's observations – what Cardijn called 'personal knowledge' – in order to build up a picture of the situation:

> First the girls would consider a particular problem in their place of employment. Next they would read a Christian social teaching bearing on the problem, and finally the group would read and reflect on a Gospel passage. Then the cell would form a plan of action which provided a Christian solution to the problem. Joseph called this his See, Judge, Act plan.[2]

The term *theological reflection* was not used of this process until much later, but it illustrates what the term means at root. Beginning with the concrete experiences and issues of the working women in their workplace, they would articulate and analyse the problem (SEE), then try to see how their faith related to the issue (JUDGE), and finally make a plan of action to transform the situation (ACT). Recent writers have offered a variety of models for understanding this same approach to Christian learning and action. Some have seen it as a process that moves through a cycle of stages (sometimes call the pastoral cycle).

Beginning with some experience or issue (experience), the group or person builds up a picture of what is going on by gathering information and perhaps looking at the experience through different lenses with the help of, for example, sociology, psychology or economics (analysis). Then, through identifying particular faith questions raised and seeking what the Bible and Christians have said in the past and present, theological reflection

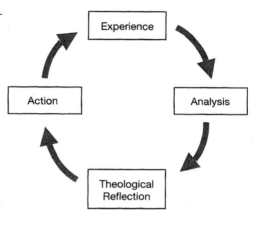

takes place (theological reflection). Then action is planned and taken, which of course leads to new experience and the cycle begins again.

One example of this is a church being offered a large cheque for some of its land by a development company eager to build a new shopping complex. At first sight this is a boon to the congregation, which is struggling to maintain its extensive premises. On further analysis, the church sees that the changing pattern of shopping in the town will make it harder for those who are least mobile and least wealthy, while meeting the needs of many of the more wealthy in the town, and the new shopping centre will simply add to this divide. Later when it is considered at the PCC, someone is asked to present a short talk on stewardship and the use of land in the Bible. Here people notice that much is said in the Old Testament about making provision for the poor in the use of the land (see, e.g., Exodus 23.11; Leviticus 19.10; Deuteronomy 15), and as a result the church asks to talk to the developer about a variety of issues to enable the less wealthy to be included. One result is the provision of a shop space at a peppercorn rent for a charity shop that will make clothes and other goods available to the least wealthy.

Another example might be a group of Christian schoolteachers who share together the tension they feel between the pressure of the system to achieve high results in school and their own intuition and professional judgement about individual children's readiness for particular developments and activities. The first appears to squeeze out the second. Over a period of time they share this together, look in detail at school policies and practice and discuss particular cases they encounter. They suggest to other each ways of working in the situation to both preserve and use their professional insight and to support the school in its desire to do well for children and parents. One suggests that God's creation and the Incarnation are relevant, in that both demonstrate God's willingness to work within but not be determined by the limitations of the world. This does not wholly resolve their dilemma, but recasting the tension in these terms helps them to understanding their situation in faith terms and to continue to work within the tension both to challenge and to be supportive within the lives of their respective schools.

A third example is of a couple who discover that the baby they are expecting is diagnosed as having Down's Syndrome. Before and after their son is born people, including church people, say to them things like, 'Never mind, they are very loving.' Clearly intending to be supportive, their friends are also revealing a view that a Down's Syndrome person is seen as somehow slightly less than human. This causes them to investigate the medical background to the syndrome and to think again about what it means to say someone is created by God and made in the image of God. In the end they discuss with their friends and their church a different way of looking at their son (and all other people with Down's Syndrome) as a person created by God and made fully in the image of God, but like the rest of us displaying some aspects of God's character in a magnified form – in his case an unaffected cheerfulness – while needing particular care and support.

Exercise 1

Can you see the four stages in each of the examples above? Try to identify in each case the four stages:

- Experience;

- Analysis;

- Theological reflection;

- Action.

Exercise 2

Think of a time in your life when your view of God changed or grew. In what way did it change? What was the trigger that prompted the change? How long did the change take? And what did you find helpful in developing your new views – for example, Bible passages, sermons, an idea from a friend? Did it make any different to your attitude and actions towards yourself, others and God?

How well does the pastoral cycle describe the stages in your changed view of God?

Summary

Theological reflection is likely to be an important part of your preparation for ministry. When people use the term they can mean a perspective – a theological way of looking at things; a skill or set of skills which enables you to identify and engage with issues from a theological point of view; or a process or model for approaching theological study of practical issues. You are likely to be engaged at some level with these three in your training. This will take some effort on your part for theological reflection is no easy task, in any of its forms. It demands both hard work and creative energy, but the purpose of this aspect of your preparation will be to strengthen your ability to recognize and respond to the presence of and purpose of God in all situations from the everyday to the global, a crucially important feature of those who minister to and lead others in the church.

Going further

Look back at the three examples given above. Can you think of other examples of such a process (of theological reflection) in your own or other people's experience? Recount the story and compare the process with the pastoral cycle. Was this the way it worked or did it work in some other way?

Further reading

Ian Aveyard, *God Thoughts: A Starter Course in Theological Reflection*, St John's Extension Studies, Chichester, 1997.

Paul H. Ballard and John Pritchard, *Practical Theology in Action*, SPCK, 1996.

Laurie Green, *Let's Do Theology*, Mowbray, 1990.

Robert L. Kinast, *What Are They Saying about Theological Reflection?*, Paulist Press, 2000.

Robert L. Kinast, *Making Faith Sense*, The Liturgical Press, 1999.

Patricia O'Connell Killen and John de Beer, *The Art of Theological Reflection*, Crossroad, 1995.

Stephen Pattison, 'Some Straw for Bricks: A Basic Introduction to Theological Reflection', *Contact* 99.2, 1989, pp. 2–9.

Part Five: Learning how to learn

13

Learning well

Starting on a programme of learning makes almost everyone nervous. Some people will not have undertaken formal learning for a long time and will worry about whether they will be able to cope. For others it will bring back bad memories of school or other previous studies in which they did not feel that things went well. Even for those who have had recent and successful experience in an academic environment, there is a small concern that it will not work out so well in the new context. Some degree of anxiety is not only common, it is natural and helpful. The essence of learning is change and this demands a willingness to be open to change: a mild level of anxiety is one of the ways we prepare ourselves for engagement with that which may change us.

Admitting any anxiety you feel is healthy too. Talking it through with a friend, your partner, the organizers of the programme or your local minister or priest can help you articulate what you are worried about and, in some cases, it will allow the basis for your worries to be challenged. For example, people are sometimes worried about age and memory. 'I can't even remember my daughter's telephone number, how am I going to learn and remember lots of new information?' The truth is, in most programmes of preparation success is not about memorization of information. It will be about being able to find, use and understand relevant information for thinking through the tasks that you will be engaged in. What is more, there is little evidence that older people cannot learn as effectively as young people. While there is some memory loss with age, this is more than compensated for by a developed ability to think and pose questions to new material, which strengthens as people age.

Likewise past academic 'failure' does not mean that you will struggle or fail. As we shall explore in this section, differences in motivation, context and styles of learning influence people's 'success' greatly. It is our consistent experience that people who at the beginning of a course see themselves as 'not good at learning', regularly discover they are deeply engaged, stimulated and surprised with their achievement. The people who encounter most difficulty are those who think they have nothing to learn!

If you are still very nervous about learning, remember that the context of all human learning is God's love forming each one of us, as we discussed in

Chapter 6. God is the one who is calling you and forming you. In your learning you are seeking to cooperate with God's calling and shaping. The God who calls you, works with you for your growth into Christ.

In this chapter we explore something about the nature of learning and how different people learn. Throughout we will make links to practical action you can take to make the most of your own capabilities and enhance your own learning. It is a longer chapter because there is a great deal to cover. You might like to tackle it in two or three sessions. There are four sections, each with several parts:

- The nature of learning;
- Factors in learning;
- Learning styles;
- Practical approaches to learning.

Use the subheadings to plan how far you will go in each session.

The nature of learning

Human learning is a highly complex business. For a little over a hundred years psychologists and educationalists have examined how it is that people learn and come up with dozens of theories and hundreds of insights. What eludes us, however, is a single theory of how people learn, and so there is no simple formula that one person can pass on to another about how to learn effectively. People learn in different ways and there are a large number of dimensions to learning, each of which can be affected by many factors. That does not mean that we know nothing more than was known a hundred years ago. We have discovered much that can inform how we design educational endeavours and how we as individuals can help ourselves learn better. Here are a few of the things that we are a little clearer on:

Learning is about change

Most definitions of learning now given by educationalists involved the word *change*. Alan Rogers describes learning as 'voluntary change in one's pattern of thinking, acting and/or feeling'. *Change* is the key word here, though Rogers emphasizes that it is a change chosen by the learner. Information may be given to us, skills shown to us and even practised by us, but without a desire to take in the new knowledge or own the skills these are unlikely to have a lasting place in our lives. In other words, learners need to be active in bringing about the change that happens.

There are different types of change

Change may be in what we know (cognitive), what we feel (affective) or what we can do (behavioural). This point is also present in the Rogers' definition above. Take, for example, Jean who volunteers to work in a support centre for asylum seekers not because she has much sympathy for asylum seekers but because the volunteer bureau she offers her time to suggests it as a local need. After several weeks she does not know much more about the facts and figures of asylum seekers, but has talked with real people and has listened to some stories. Her emotions have been stirred, and her views about asylum seekers, the way newspapers report on the issue, and those who want to make political capital out of people's fears of 'mass immigration' have also changed. Jean may not *know* much more about the subject but has changed her attitude to it.

Learning can take place with or without teaching and education

Teaching and education are dependent on the human ability to learn, not the other way round as we sometimes think. Teaching is an attempt to bring about learning, and education is the organization of policies, structures and activities for learning to occur. Good teaching and education will facilitate learning but, as we pointed out above, learning is primarily in the hands of the learner. It cannot be done to you without your cooperation to some degree. What is more, people learn all sorts of things from their own experience and research outside educational structures and without teachers.

All these points are relevant to beginning any course of study and provoke some reflection for embarking on a preparation for ministry programme. First, you need to be actively engaged in your own learning and the more active you are, the more effective will be the learning. Second, you should expect and work with change. The change will almost certainly be in the knowledge you have, but equally it may involve both your skills and attitudes. People often underestimate the emotional component of learning but it is very real, especially in the Christian context, where growth in virtues such as love, forgiveness, humility and kindness provides perhaps the most obvious signs of our growing to be more Christ-like. Finally, while your learning will be driven and shaped by the programme and its teaching, you can utilize resources within and beyond the course and take your learning further by your own research and explorations.

Factors in learning

Learning is affected by a variety of factors. This is the area where we have made most progress in understanding learning, but because there are many factors combined in one person or group, we cannot always tell which will be the dominant factors. Here are some. For sake of convenience I am categorizing them under four headings.

Physical factors

We encounter the world through our senses – touch, taste, sight, hearing and smell – at least in the first instance. Our learning is clearly influenced by the way our senses apprehend things. It is still surprising to me how much in my memory is associated with a taste or an odour and what powerful memories are evoked by these senses. Clearly, if any of our senses are impaired or highly developed this will affect learning. It also means that our learning may be more effective if several of our senses are engaged at once. You are more likely to remember a Shakespearian play you acted in than one you simply read because more of you was involved physically. Likewise, the physical circumstances of your learning environment can make a difference. Simple things like the right amount of light, heat and comfort will make a difference. Of course, being uncomfortable can also aid some types of learning. Sitting alongside those attending relatives in an Accident and Emergency hospital on a Friday night, or meeting a prisoner in her cell, is not comfortable but may lead to very significant reflection and learning. Physical factors needs to be taken seriously in our learning.

Here are some practical suggestions about enhancing your learning through attention to the physical factors:

- If you have an impairment, make it known in the institution or group with which you are studying. Recent legislation (The Special Educational Needs and Disability Acts 2001) requires action to make equal learning opportunities for all, and provision of resources for those with impairments. Induction loops, large-print handouts and taping facilities are not uncommon and certainly not unreasonable requests.

- Be active in relation to the physical environment of your learning. If you are going to be in a teaching room for some time, make sure there is good ventilation, light, appropriate heat, comfortable seats and good surfaces to take notes. If not, ask what can be done to make it better and offer constructive suggestions. The same is true of where you do your own personal study – make it a place where you can work well.

- Utilize your senses in your encounters and reflect on them. For example, if you are keeping a journal, record sights, sounds, smells and feelings in your jottings. When you come to reread and reflect on experiences recorded in this way, the richness of the sense record may help to make the memory more vivid and insight more readily forthcoming.

- In your presentations, whether writing essays, leading seminars, or leading worship, remember the senses. I (Roger) can strongly recall the impact of someone leading a session on liberation theology drawing on his experience of living in Latin America and using two crosses which were passed around. One was smooth, polished and felt comfortable in the hands. It had been made by a church organization and sold to worshippers. The other was rough in feel and rugged, even slightly ugly in appearance. It was made by poor people in a base community and given to members as a sign of their own believing and commitment. The second deeply reflected the experience of the people and the God in whom they found hope.

Mental factors

Our brains are large and impenetrably complex. We do not yet understand how they work in detail but it is clear that our brains are involved in how we receive information, how we process it and store it, and how we respond to situations. They are also involved in the motivation we feel for learning and in what we perceive as barriers. Our brains have to be actively involved in constructing knowledge and the way they seem to do this, especially in more complex learning, is to do with making meaning – storing information that we link together in some sort of coherent way. Crucial to effective learning programmes is that there are ways which allow people to link new ideas to previous experience, with time and opportunities for learners to construct their own meaning.

Here are some practical suggestions about enhancing your learning through attention to the mental factors:

- Be clear about your motivation, set yourself goals, discuss them with your tutor and remind yourself of your goals regularly.

- Be active in the way you engage with new ideas. Ask questions, take notes, make your own links with other ideas and experience and discuss these with others. Do not assume that the handout, however good, means you don't need to take notes or think about the subject for yourself.

- Develop a healthy lifestyle that supports study. You will work better if you have exercise, rest and social activity. Your brain may well keep working at things in the background when you are involved in recreation.

- Practise reflection. Revisit your notes and written work and ask questions of the material. You may have to do this, if examinations are to be taken. One of the continuing values of exams is that in revision people begin to see new meanings and make connections. If you don't have examinations, it is all the more worthwhile to go over things and reflect on the ideas and implications.

- Share issues of difficulty and changes of life circumstances with those who lead the course. Some things will affect the way you work all the time (such as dyslexia) and need to be addressed with the right learning resources. Others may have some short-term immediate effect (such as an illness which lasts a couple of weeks), but will demand much emotional and mental energy for a period.

Social factors

You only need to observe children with their friends to see that peers influence behaviour, language, interests and attitudes. Adults as well as children are constantly affected by their social interaction with others. We observe and repeat behaviour, our views are often modified by our discussions with others, we tend to conform to the values and outlook of groups to which we belong and we learn ways of acting within certain types of community. When we add to that the influence of the newspapers, TV and radio we recognize that our learning is socially conditioned to a significant degree. The social factors can be either positive or negative. Working with others may increase the possibility of learning, discussing with others can develop our ability to reflect and yield deeper insight than might be achieved on our own. On the other hand, conformity may inhibit critical thinking and poor role models replicate poor practice.

Here are some practical suggestions about enhancing your learning through attention to the social factors:

- Utilize the communities to which you belong. During your programme you will be part of several communities and these may change over the period of the training. Talk with peers, placement contacts, church friends, work colleagues and members of other communities to which you belong. They can be part of the learning experience. Compare and discuss different experiences and perceptions. Make time for reflection in any collaborative tasks and ask for help when you need it.

- Makes good use of any mentors provided. 'Old hands' usually have much wisdom to share and the better ones will help you think through problems by posing questions and offering relevant experience without solving the issue for you. Some of the best mentoring systems in learning are set up by and for the students themselves: a buddy system.

- Be aware of the role models in your institution and learning settings. Who do you respond well to or admire, and why? Whom would you want to imitate? These are good questions to pursue but don't be afraid of critical reflection too. It is possible to see where someone's approach or action falls short and what alternatives might be utilized, while respecting that person.

- Be prepared to stand back from both the groups to which you belong and even the institutions as a whole to ask questions about how things operate and why. What are the assumptions behind the structure and pattern of the institution's working, and what is the underlying theology? This need not be a cynical criticism. If explored in dialogue with others in the group and institution, it can provide a creative way of countering unhelpful hegemonies that can take over.

Contextual factors

There was a time when theorists assumed that learning was the same everywhere for everyone, for men, for women and for children, and in whatever country and culture they happened to live. More and more research suggests that this is not so. Location is important, as is the cultural and historical context of particular groups. Not only are women and men biologically different, but in many cultures their life experiences and cultural history have been vastly different. Recent work on Christian education for black young people suggests that their cultural and historical contexts are different from those of white young people in the same countries and so learning and education need to be developed differently. Research also shows that learning and context are very closely connected. For example, street children in South America often develop sophisticated mathematical skills in dealing with currency exchange with tourists but cannot perform the same operations when presented with similar problems in schools. Cultural differences between countries in the West and Asian countries have also been shown to affect how people learn.

Here are some practical suggestions about enhancing your learning through attention to the contextual factors:

- Ask questions about the contexts you are engaged with. This includes work, church and study settings. Find out how things came to be as they are and why they continue to work in particular ways. This is the first step to change and development.

- Explore the contextual aspects of what you study. This applies as much to New Testament study as to the churches in which you lead worship or the communities in which you are engaged in mission. To make sense of a biblical text you need to explore its original setting as much as you can and equally take account of your own context and why and in what way you are studying the text.

- Accept that there are different ways of approaching a subject. According to some research women's thinking may be different and develop in different ways from that of men. People's thinking and the way they express faith will be affected significantly by the stage of life they have reached. Take time to listen and understand how this works with different people, and why. It will deepen your own learning.

- Work at transferring knowledge and skill from one part of your life and work to another. This does not happen automatically – far from it. You need to bring newfound knowledge, skills and attitudes into other communities and work out how they affect who you are and what you do. This is another good opportunity for reflection!

Pause for thought

Take a few moments to write down a list of practical points from the above sections that you want to remember to help your own learning.

Learning styles

In recent years there are has been a tendency among educationalists to talk about different 'learning styles'. Underlying this approach is the theory that the combination of genetic inheritance with our life experience creates our temperament and shapes our personality. Our personality and temperament in turn predispose us to certain ways of learning. All people do not learn in the same way. Rather we learn in different ways and education needs to take account of this in order to be effective. Now this would be an impossible task if it meant that each individual should be treated separately and exclusively. Most theorists, however, have suggested that people can be grouped into types, and these types have a degree of consistency. By knowing your own learning style it may be possible to work in ways that best utilize your natural strengths and to think through how to tackle teaching that does not suit your preferred learning style.

The questions then posed for us are: 'What are the different learning styles?'; 'What are their characteristics?' and 'How do they relate to learning?' There are various attempts to answer these questions. We look briefly at three.

The Honey and Mumford learning styles

David Kolb identified four learning styles[1]:

ACTIVISTS throw themselves enthusiastically into any new activity. They like the challenge of new experiences but are bored with implementation and long-term consolidation. Their watchword is 'Try anything once!' They learn best when they are in the thick of things.

REFLECTORS like to stand back and ponder experiences, observing them from different perspectives. They collect and analyse data before coming to conclusions. They don't like to be put on the spot or asked for immediate answers. Their motto is 'Look before you leap.' They learn best when they have time to reflect, prepare and think about experience.

THEORISTS like to analyse and synthesize facts and observations into coherent theories. They think through problems in a logical way and prefer the rational and objective to the subjective. A central question for them is 'Is this idea coherent and does it stand up to interrogation?' They learn best when they can see the whole picture and how it holds together.

PRAGMATISTS are keen on trying out ideas, theories and techniques to see if they work in practice. They are practical problem solvers and want to know 'Does it work?' They learn best when they can see that their learning will have an impact on what they do and are often motivated to learn by the practical payoff they see at the end.

Pause for thought

How would you describe your own preferred learning style?

Write down the category you think best describes your preferred style of learning. What in your past experience of learning suggests this to you?

Peter Honey and Alan Mumford, British educationalists, developed this idea further by designing a test to identify one's preferred learning style. The Honey and Mumford learning styles test enables people to discover their own and others' preferred learning style. The answers that individuals give to a questionnaire indicate to what degree those answering fit each category. While we all have some aspects of each style within our personalities and there are times and contexts when one style will be more evident, nevertheless, we generally have a learning style preference and this can be discerned from the questionnaire answers. (If you wanted to do a form of the test for yourself, you can use the short version of it found in Yvonne Craig's book recommended in the Further reading section).

The Myers–Briggs Type Indicator (MBTI®)

The Myers–Briggs Type Indicator takes its names from the mother and daughter team that developed the original psychometric test, Katharine Cook Briggs and

Isabel Briggs Myers. They based their work on the ideas of the psychologist Carl G. Jung (1875–1961) and, prompted by World War II and the desire to understand conflict and avoid waste in human lives, they developed the Indicator to be a way of giving people information about their personality type. It was thought that understanding how conflict arises and why people sometimes cannot work together because of personality would help avoid both quarrelling and perhaps even war. It is used widely. Something like 3.5 million people take the MBTI® test each year and it has been translated into 30 or more languages.

The basis of the MBTI® is the idea that there are fundamentally different ways our personalities can be structured. For example, we can be either extrovert or introvert. This means that we either draw our energy primarily from other people or primarily from within ourselves. Extroverts need to be in contact and communication with others to be energized, whereas introverts need peace, quiet and time away from others to refresh themselves. There is, of course, a spectrum. Some people are more extrovert than others, some more introverted, and so on. The MBTI® test measures where you are on the axis between extreme extrovert and extreme introvert. You are to some degree an extrovert or an introvert. Neither is good or bad, they are simply different personality traits within normal behaviour. You can see immediately, however, how this might affect learning. Extroverts are likely to learn more effectively in a group, introverts may prefer to have books and tackle essay writing.

Introvert–Extrovert is one of four axes in the MBTI® structure. The others are:

- **Sensing or Intuitive:** How do you gather information? Is it from hard data (facts, figures, dates, etc.), or through seeing the connections and relationships in the big picture?

- **Thinking or Feeling:** How do you process and resolve issues? Which is more important to you when making decisions – whether logic and common sense are applied, or how things feel?

- **Perceiving or Judging:** How do you deal with the outside world? Do you prefer to live flexibly, spontaneously and act on the spur of the minute, or do you give attention to organizing yourself carefully through planning, lists and timetables?

Introvert (I)	....	Extrovert (E)
Sensing (S)	....	Intuitive (N)
Thinking (T)	....	Feeling (F)
Perceiving (P)	....	Judging (J)

Essentially, the test asks you describe yourself through agreeing or disagreeing with various statements. These questions are designed to determine whether you are I or E, S or N, T or F and P or J. (People are only very rarely on the border between two options.) Putting these together give you a personality profile. If you are good at maths, you will have worked out there are 16 different possible outcomes (e.g., one person may be ENFP and another ISFJ, and so on). The particular configuration of elements describes your key characteristics and inclinations and may indicate a lot about how you relate to your marriage partner and children, what kind of work colleague you are, how you might learn most effectively and what worship and approach to prayer will suit you. It is also helpful in determining why you might clash with someone else, and for this reason it is used extensively in helping teams of people who work together to understand each other and get the best out of their team.

It is not uncommon for courses of preparation for ministry to include an MBTI® exercise. These are non-threatening events and most people enjoy taking part and discussing their personality profile. The tests are normally run by qualified testers, who can help you think about the implications of your personality for study, group dynamics, prayer life and worship.

The theory of multiple intelligences

In the early days of IQ tests, it was assumed that intelligence was a single and fixed capacity within human beings, and once you underwent an IQ test and were given an IQ rating, this was the key measure of your general intelligence and academic ability. Over the years this idea has been challenged in a number of ways. The influential North American educationalist Howard Gardner presents one of the more recent challenges. Gardner suggests that rather than one single intelligence we have seven different capacities or intelligences and we are differently able in these spheres of intelligence. Gardner came to this theory of multiple intelligences through research on brain-damaged and non-brain-damaged children, which suggested that it is possible to lose capacities in one or two areas and still be as competent as before in others. Thus they not only represent what may be labelled differing abilities, but are embedded in separate and different cognitive processes underlying these intelligences.

The seven intelligences are:

- **Language or linguistic intelligence:** ability in learning and using language, e.g. in a poet or writer.

- **Logical-mathematical intelligence:** ability with number and patterns, e.g. in a scientist.

- **Spatial intelligence:** ability in seeing and using space, colour and design, e.g. in a painter, architect or engineer.

- **Musical/rhythmic intelligence:** ability in music and musical patterns, e.g. in a musician or songwriter.

- **Bodily/kinaesthetic intelligence:** ability to use one's body and movement, e.g. in a fine athlete, dancer or surgeon or craftworker.

- **Interpersonal intelligence:** ability to understand and relate to others, e.g. in a good salesperson or teacher.

- **Intrapersonal intelligence:** ability to know one's own desires, fears and competencies, and to act productively on the basis of that knowledge, e.g. in a wise counsellor or leader.

As with the Honey and Mumford learning styles, one can see that individuals are going to learn most effectively when engaging in learning in ways that suit their particular strengths. But you might say that some kinds of learning just are simply not suited to preparation for ministry or the tasks that ministers carry out. This may be true in part, but it may also be the case that we have not imagined other ways of learning particular material. As an example let us take Bible study. For a long time if you went to a church Bible study in almost any denomination you would have encountered a similar approach which would have been some verbal input by a group leader, perhaps followed by reflection and discussion by members of the group and prayers at the end. We now recognize that there are a variety of ways of getting into Bible study. Barbara Bruce has taken on the theory of multiple intelligences in a creative way and has produced two books which are designed to help people design and lead Bible studies according to the particular intelligence strengths of participants.[2] She demonstrates that the same passage might be tackled in seven very different ways. What is true for studying the Bible may also be true for other forms of learning too.

Your learning style and learning

What can we learn from these various theories about learning styles? At first glance it can be bewildering. Which of these theories is right? Are they connected together, and if so, how? How do I know which to use to help me in my learning or in planning learning for others? These are common questions and are not easily answered. However, there a few generic thoughts that can be useful for those (re)entering formal study or preparation for ministry programmes.

First, you are going be more at home with some aspects of the course than others. If you recognize yourself as a pragmatist you will probably be most at home when you are learning things that you can see will make a difference in your life and work. You will look forward to these aspects of the course and be engaged with them. If you are extrovert you will enjoy the discussions and group work but be less attracted to time on your own with an essay title. Knowing this can help you be more disciplined about the things that are not so attractive or comfortable.

Second, many topics can be tackled in different ways. As was suggested with Bible study, there may be several ways of tackling a particular subject and you can be proactive in negotiating your own assignments. For example, it is possible to look at the person of Christ by examination of the Scriptures, the writing and debates of the Church and modern written accounts. It is also possible to explore this by looking at paintings of Christ through the centuries and from different parts of the world. If you have a strong interest or expertise in the second you may be able to combine the two to some extent in a piece of work and give focus to your reading and note taking. Most institutions are open to negotiation provided it is manageable and achievable within the frame of time and assessment structures. Most tutors will recognize that people who come with ideas are likely to be more effective in their learning.

Third, where some forms of learning are not your preferred style, you may need to allow more time and work harder at those aspects which require you to engage in a different way. None of the theories of learning styles suggests that you should never undertake learning in ways which are not your preferred style. Indeed, most would say that working in your less preferred styles for some of the time may be very productive. You may, however, need to spend more time on such tasks. Because you do not like them you may be tempted to leave them to the end of your agenda. There is a good case for doing exactly the opposite, making sure you plan well in advance, allow a good deal of time, and prioritize this over aspects of the work that you prefer. Thus where there is a choice about how to explore a subject you need to think carefully what will be of most benefit to you in your growth and development. Being aware of your learning style may help you make hard decisions too.

Pause for thought

Take a few moments to identify half a dozen aspects of your own learning style. Where are your strengths and what is your preferred approach?

What do you think this will mean in the learning on your course?

Practical approaches to learning

Finally there are some very practical points about learning in the context of preparation for ministry that may be useful to note.

Organize your timetable

In whatever form you are studying – part-time combined with full-time work, a weekly group meeting, or full-time residential training – the demands of study will be great. Building a rhythm of study within and alongside other responsibilities and commitments takes time and thoughtful planning. Ask tutors for an estimate in hours per week terms of the time you will need to read, do assignments, and engage in practical work, and so on. Estimates are hard to give because people work at different rates in some of these areas. However, when you have this figure add another 30 per cent and then see how that will fit into your week. What evenings, days, or hours per day do you need to designate for it? Then talk it through with family or friends with who you share a significant amount of your time. It will affect them too and their support will be vital to your successful learning. Determine when deadlines are and write these into your diary, then plan dates sometime before the deadlines by which you will have drafted your essay or completed your preparation for a practical activity. This allows you to reread and reflect on what you have done and almost always results in a better piece of work. When you are under way with the studies review your timetable in the light of the actual work and revise accordingly. When you have a pattern established, stick to it.

Learn strategically

Some research work in Scandinavia[3] concluded that there were two types of learning, surface and deep learning. Surface learning was characterized as learning facts, dates, views and processes. This was employed by many students who were fine if their examination or essay title allowed them to reproduce what they had memorized, but otherwise they had considerable difficulty, especially in using their knowledge to tackle problems that they had not encountered before. Deep learning was, by contrast, characterized by the desire of the student to understand the underlying principles and ideas and how issues related together. These students were much better at applying knowledge to new situations.

There was, however, in further research work, a third category of student learning that was more successful still and it was named strategic learning. This is basically a combination of deep learning with a careful eye to what was required by the institutions. Strategic learners looked carefully at assessment criteria, required presentation style, word limits and so on, and made sure that their deep learning was channelled into the form that was expected. Now that much energy goes into assessment criteria and these have to be made available to students, it is important to read and address these in your work. We will look at this in more detail in the section on assessment.

Foster reflection

We have referred elsewhere to the nature of reflection. According to Jennifer Moon[4] reflection is a particular form of thinking that is often prompted by problems requiring people to revisit knowledge they already have. As they revisit their knowledge, often they reorder it and develop new insights. As you work on any study – taking notes, writing essays, making journals or engaging in practical work – there is also the 'problem' of how this fits with your previous experience and views and what you are training for. We need to ask also: what does it say about God, Church, vocation, mission and ministry? Regular reflection, be it on your own, as you read, in prayerful quietness, or in discussion with others, will be an important part of channelling your learning in Christian growth and development.

Work collaboratively

We have mentioned here and in Chapter 6 on formation, the importance of other people in your learning. Conversations, the sharing of ideas and resources, challenges to consider other views, pastoral support and encouragement, these are all the benefits of being a learning community. Peers, mentors and tutors share the journey with you, so use these people resources as part of your learning and become part of their learning resource too. This is not simply about being an effective learner, it is fundamental to the essence of God's calling to be the Church. As the writer to the Ephesians puts it:

> But speaking the truth in love, we must grow up in every way into him who is the head, into Christ, from whom the whole body, joined and knit together by every ligament with which it is equipped, as each part is working properly, promotes the body's growth in building itself up in love. (Ephesians 4.15-16)

It is the whole body working together in the practice and pursuit of truth in love that makes for the growth of the Church into Christ.

This community dimension is also the way to avoid being isolated when things get difficult with study, which they do for most people at some time. When you can't meet the deadline or don't understand the ideas or can't grasp the skill, there are others who are in this with you and who will be willing to talk it through and support you in solving the difficulty.

Going further

1. Look back on your good and bad experiences of learning. What were the factors that helped or hindered your learning?

2.   Ask your friends to describe their learning style to you. How do they learn most effectively? Ask them to tell you what they think your learning style is, and why.

3.   Make yourself a checklist of ways to develop your own learning, using this chapter. Make it is short and simple, so that you can return to it regularly.

Further reading

Alice Airburst and Lisa Airburst, *Effective Teaching, Effective Learning: Making the Personality Connection in your Classroom*, Davies-Black Publishing, 1995.

Barbara Bruce, *7 Ways of Teaching the Bible to Children*, Abingdon, 1996.

Barbara Bruce, *7 Ways of Teaching the Bible to Adults*, Abingdon, 2000.

Yvonne Craig, *Learning for Life: A Handbook of Adult Religious Education*, Mowbray, 1994.

Leslie Francis, *Personality Type and Scripture*, Mowbray, 1997.

14

Assessment and learning

(How to write your first assignment)

'Will there be exams?' is one of the questions people often ask (or want to ask but are not sure whether they should) when meeting those who will be leading their course of study. For some there is a particular fear of examinations which deep down they believe to be designed to catch people out, make them fail and look foolish. But even where there are no such examinations – and there are very few courses in preparation for ministry which use this form of assessment – most people feel a little nervous about the fact that someone will be assessing them. There are, however, good reasons for assessment. In this chapter we explore some of those reasons, particularly in the Christian Church context, alert you to what to expect, and suggest ways of working well within an assessment structure. We also offer guidelines on how to write your first assignment. It may seem an obvious point, but we have called the chapter 'Assessment and learning' deliberately: the different ways in which you are assessed will each contribute to what you can learn.

Assessment: who needs to know and why?

In our context, assessment is asking 'How you are getting on with your preparation for ministry?' Who might need to know this and why? There are a number of people who need to know.

You

You need to know so as to be more effective in learning. If you know what is going well you can use the information to reinforce and strengthen your learning. If you see you are progressing, it can build confidence and you can go on to tackle new challenges. Assessing where you have got to can also help you measure and plan your progress through a programme. Equally if you know where your mistakes are or you can identify where you are not quite grasping things, you can begin to address the problems. With good assessment and feedback you can improve your learning.

Your tutor

Your tutor or course leader needs to know, so as to decide how best to help you. If she or he is aware of your progress, it may help your tutor to monitor the pace of work set, to identify topics for discussion and to provide the right kind of teaching. The Latin root of the word assessment is *assidere* meaning 'to sit alongside'. A key role for a tutor is to sit alongside you to get to know you well and to help you develop. This can only be done on the basis of a good relationship and accurate information about your progress.

Your programme designers and leaders

The people who plan and run the course need to know. They may need to know in order to satisfy a validating university that standards are being achieved, or in order to report to the relevant church body. Another use of assessment information is to measure the effectiveness of the programme. If things are not working well it may point to poor teaching or a weak process, which needs to be modified or changed.

Your church

Your church, local or national, needs to know so as to estimate whether and when you will be able to take a full part in its ministry. If your ministry is to be exercised on behalf of the Church, the Church needs to have confidence in your ability as well as calling to do the work. To do this it must make some kind of evaluation of your learning and growth towards ministry. For the Church, assessment can provide a way of reporting achievement, estimating aptitude for new learning, identifying readiness for responsibility, or give evidence for a character reference.

Your family and friends

Your family and friends need to know how you are getting on so as to be able to support, encourage and pray for you. They may in fact not need or want to see your marks for assignments or the feedback on your practical work. They will be more interested in how you feel about the studies – whether you like the people who teach, are stimulated by the things you are learning, and what the challenges are for you. If you have a support group, there may be scheduled time to share a new experience you have gone through, a new idea that has excited you, or a problem you are facing. If there is no formal arrangement of this kind, it may be your spouse or children, parents, or church friends who share the experience with you. You will be the main source of information for this group, rather than a report or printed marks, but what you share will be informed in some ways by the assessment processes of the programme.

For all these very practical reasons some measurement of your progress is both helpful and necessary. There is a broader Christian framework in which to look at the idea of assessment.

Assessment and Christian faith

Surprising as it may seem, assessment is an idea found in the Bible. Indeed the concepts of judgement and measurement run throughout the Scriptures. While the main emphasis is on God as judge, the idea of assessing and making judgements of ourselves and others within the compass of God's calling is a frequent theme.

Check it out

Look at the following texts and reflect on the reasons for and ways of judging in them:

- Leviticus 19.15
- Deuteronomy 1.16
- Isaiah 11.3-4
- Matthew 18.15
- Acts 5.1-10
- 1 Corinthians 14.29
- 1 Thessalonians 5.21

God gives to human beings the capacity to reason, create, choose and enter into dialogue with each other. This is a special kind of freedom and God holds us responsible for the choices we make. St Paul encourages us to have a true and sober estimate of ourselves (Romans 12.3) and to weigh the gifts of others (1 Corinthians 14.29) so that the body benefits and Christ is honoured. This is a form of assessment which serves a purpose in reality, saving people from self-delusion and enabling the taking of personal responsibility. If structured well and within a context of truth and love, assessment can create ways of being accountable for our discipleship, discerning our vocation and nurturing human consciousness and self-esteem.

Remember too that this is not just something that happens to individuals in training. Accountability as a part of the Christian calling needs to go on in some form all through our lives. Some of that assessment will be by people in authority, but much more of it will be undertaken in a form of self-assessment and with others on the same journey.

The Church too needs assessment. It also is called and must be judged against God's character, kingdom and mission. In order to do this, Churches have evolved ways of assessing and developing their life and witness. In many dioceses there are 'church audits' or 'visitation schemes' which are ways of helping churches to look at their lives to see how they are getting on in mission. In recent years a similar approach has been developed in the Methodist Church under the title of *Pilgrim's Way*. In all these approaches the basis idea is to hold up a mirror to our corporate life and look at the mirror alongside God's call to the Church, so as to see where to go and what to do next.

The scope and range of assessment

Within a programme of study and preparation for ministry, there will most probably be two different but related frames of assessment. Academic assessment may well be linked to a validation or accreditation structure. That is, you may receive a certificate, diploma or degree awarded, validated or recognized by a university or other formal educational structure such as the Open College Network. For this award to have meaning and status within the wider world, the assessed work must be judged to reach a certain standard and there will be requirements made by the validating body to ensure this.

For most people in programmes of preparation for ministry, assessment is also made by the Church. It will have its own structures and processes for assessing a person's readiness and ability, in which the validated qualification will be only one part. For example, local preachers in training for the Methodist Church currently undertake a study programme in which there are essays and other assignments to be completed, assessed local by a tutor and moderated nationally. This programme of studies has been recognized by several universities. However, completing the study programme in itself would not qualify a person to be a local preacher within the Methodist Church. For this recognition the local circuit has an assessment role in judging the person's quality of preaching and leading of worship over a period of time, usually alongside the study programme, and the final decision to admit someone as a local preacher will be taken by the Circuit Meeting. Likewise, those in training for ordained ministry in the Church of England, the Methodist Church or United Reformed Church not only study for academic awards as a key part of their training but are subject to reports, interviews and others processes that the Church sets up and operates to assess a person's suitability.

Assessment structures need to be appropriate, fair and rigorous. They need to be appropriate in that they need to be suitable to test what it is that needs to be tested. Suppose you want to train pastoral carers to work on behalf of the Church. How would you assess whether people were ready at the end of the course to do this work? Setting an essay on 'how to support someone through bereavement' will tell you some things about the person's understanding of loss and the stages of grief, but it might not tell whether the person can build rapport with people, whether she or he is a good listener and can keep necessary confidentiality, and whether the person can spot the signs of when professional help is needed. You might like to think how these things might be assessed, so that the Church could have confidence that the person it was commissioning to do this in its name was ready, able and suitable.

Pause for thought

How would you assess the readiness of the pastoral carer to work on behalf of the Church?

In trying to imagine what assessment would be appropriate to our pastoral carer's training, you probably thought that it needs to relate to what they will actually do when in ministry. That is, someone needs to see them in action – doing what pastoral carers do in real situations. Now this has implications for teaching and learning. If you think that a good way of assessing our pastoral carer candidate, might be to see the person in action in real visiting situations, you will need to find someone who could be alongside them, perhaps an experienced carer, who could make a judgement about the qualities and skills we named above.

This has various implications, but supposing we can organize it, there is then another question to consider. How are we going to be sure that the assessor's judgement of this person is the same as that of another assessor's of another person? Could it be that a trainee carer might be judged to be fine by one assessor and failed by another? We need some monitoring system to ensure consistency. This brings us back to the words *fair* and *rigorous*. Assessment systems and patterns need to fair by being consistent for all learners, and rigorous in testing extensively enough to be reasonably sure of making an accurate judgement.

These different aspects of assessment – appropriateness, on the one hand, and fairness and rigour, on the other – are sometimes in tension. A simple example of this would be children's reading tests. If children are asked to read isolated words, free of context, the test is fair and rigorous. You can test lots of children and the test is the same for each. But reading is a contextual activity where reading sentences in a story structure affects meaning. Moreover, a child reading to someone in whom they have confidence (a well-known teacher or parent) is more likely to be relaxed and confident so that their true reading ability is shown. But once you use particular books or certain kinds of stories and introduce significant adults you reduce the reliability by increasing the factors that could be different for each child.

What this means in our context is that there has to be careful thought given to assessment in order for it to be as effective as possible. It also means that there are many different patterns of assessment now operating in educational environments as people attempt to develop assessment processes that are both valid and reliable.

Different types of assessment

Here are a few of the assessment patterns that you might encounter in a preparation for ministry course.

Type	Example	Useful for
Assessment of 'performance in situ'	A preacher preaching in church	Assessing integration of skills, knowledge and attitudes in context
Assessed written work	An essay on themes in John's Gospel	Assessing research, thinking and writing skills
Self-assessment	Watching and evaluating a video of oneself leading worship	Developing self-reflection skills
Peer-assessment	Report by others on your part in a group mission	Developing and assessing self-knowledge and feedback skills
Assessed interview or conversation	A simulated pastoral encounter	Testing how quickly and well people think and act on the spot
Portfolio building	A collection of evidence to show administrative ability	Assessing prior experience and competence of person in complex or diverse jobs
Report from supervisor or mentor	A placement report	Learning how your character and skills are seen by an experienced person
Summary report from tutor or course leader	Report to diocesan director of ordination, Connexional committee or bishop	Drawing together evidence from a variety of assessed contexts to present a whole picture of person's character and development

Unseen written examinations	Translating a New Testament Greek text	Assessing transferable skills and the ability to use knowledge and skill in unfamiliar setting
Assessed seminar	Leading a 40-minute session on a given topic	Assessing education and communication skills as well as research and thinking ability

This is simply a list of some possibilities. There are many more patterns of assessment and a huge variety of combinations in some courses.

Pause for thought

What experience do you have of being assessed – e.g., from school, work, learning to drive?

Which of the above methods of being assessed have you experienced? Were the assessment methods suitable to the purpose of the learning?

Learning outcomes and assessment criteria

The key to both good course design and assessment is having clear learning outcomes for a course or course module. A learning outcome is what someone is expected to know, be able to do or feel, or what qualities or characteristics are to be demonstrated at the end of the period of formation, study and assessment. Thus the key to making the most of the learning is to examine the learning outcomes and keep them in mind as you study. This will help you see where you are going and how best to get there.

At the time of writing, the Methodist Church, the United Reformed Church and the Church of England are developing the idea of training lay and local preachers together with lay Readers. One of the first stages of doing has been to identify the outcomes of any training for these three similar ministries. In the first document draft these were divided into *knowledge outcomes* – e.g., knowledge about the Bible, its content and ways of reading and interpreting it; *competence outcomes* – e.g., skills in leading worship, such as preaching and leading prayers in public worship; and *formational outcomes* – e.g., a developing personal prayer life and an appreciation of the spirituality of others. These learning outcomes portray what a Reader, lay or local preacher needs to know, to be, and to be able to do. In formational preparation for this ministry one is working towards developing all these within oneself.

Assessment criteria are a set of standards against which work is to be judged. They are usually published in course handbooks and are extremely useful in planning and preparing your work for assessment. They should be obviously related to the learning outcomes, they should be appropriate for the particular methods of assessment used and should indicate clearly what assessors are looking for in high-quality work.

Assessment criteria are often written using particular terms. For written or orally assessed work key words include:

- **Describe** – means accurately to outline an idea or sequence of events using your own words.

- **Understand** – often means to describe something in your own words *and* show that you can relate it to other views or ideas you have met or already hold. In other words, to show that you have grasped the details and coherence of the notion and its implications.

- **Apply** – means to take an idea and use it appropriately to another situation or context.

- **Evaluate** – means to weigh up the strengths and weakness of an idea or position and come to you own judgement using argument and evidence to support your view. Alternatively, it may mean judging between two or more different interpretations, again using argument and evidence.

In the meaning of these four assessment words there is a degree of overlap. Certainly demonstrating understanding involves some description, but also going further. Application and evaluation depend on good understanding or they cannot be achieved. On the whole most tasks, whether essays, examinations or other forms of assessment, will want you to press beyond the first two to the 'higher' skills of application and evaluation.

Another key word in relation to assessment is the word *critical*. *Critical* does not mean negative faultfinding, but rather points to the ability to examine statements and ideas carefully and not simply take them at their face value. It means looking at the evidence and argument to see whether they are strong, discerning the assumptions that lie behind a view, testing the logic and implications of an idea and considering alternative interpretations. A critical evaluation will examine whether the idea stands up to various tests and is thus coherent and convincing. Only by learning to be critical can you improve your ability to think clearly and be consistent in your ideas and work. Reason is not everything, but developing your critical faculties will be an important side of preparation for ministry.

Feedback on the work you do is a key part of the process of assessment. This is where the information is for you and your learning. Good feedback (written or oral or both) will be marked by its usefulness in helping you develop your work. It will be set out in terms of the assessment criteria and should help you see where your work is strong as well as what you need to do to improve. If you do not understand what is being said, ask as soon as possible while the work is still fresh, and look at the feedback again when tackling the next similar assignment.

Reporting

Assessment via report writing will usually be more broadly based than academic assessment criteria. Reports will address the wider learning outcomes that the Church requires of people involved in the particular ministry to which you feel called. For example, those responsible for making decisions will want to know about such things as the quality of your relationships, your prayer life, your leadership, as well as your grasp of mission and your ability to think and write.

It is normal in most settings for you to have some part in this assessment. This may take the form of your writing a self-assessment, and/or discussing the draft report with the person asked to write it. Your involvement is crucial. Self-assessment will cause you to think back over your studies, reflect on your personal journey, and help you become more aware of what has changed, how you have grown and perhaps where you need to do more work. This is valuable in itself but it also helps in creating a habit of self-assessment and reflection that can continue throughout your ministry.

One of the guidelines in all report writing is that opinions and comments must be based on evidence and that evidence should be cited in the report. That is useful for your own self-assessment too. If you think you have grown in knowledge, skill, attitude or character, what evidence can you point to that supports your view?

Data protection

Legislation means that people cannot keep reports or formal assessment secret from you. In most institutions all reports and other formal assessment will be shown to you and they may well be discussed with you as they are written. You will probably have an opportunity to comment on reports, and you may well be asked to write a self-assessment alongside the institutional report. If you want to see the contents of any file with information or comments made about you, you can ask to see it. There will be an agreed and public procedure in place for access.

Assessment is for life. Get used to it!

Don't make the mistake of thinking that when the course or programme is over there will be no more assessment. It may take different forms but assessment will continue over the whole of your work and ministry in some form. Some of the assessment will be informal and casual – what someone tells you about the sermon you preached or the support you gave. Alongside that, there will be structures and processes for assessment built in by the Church or church agencies related to your vocation. For example, there may an appraisal system and/or a continuing development or education expectation. You may be required or choose to have a supervisor or consultant to ensure support and accountability, and there may be references written about your work and personal qualities in relation to a job application. All these are a form of assessment. Good systems will help you continue to deepen your knowledge of yourself, your work and your context, to develop your strengths and to be more effective in your calling.

Writing your first essay

It is not possible here to outline how to approach every form of assessment, but on the assumption that most courses will involve essay writing, we offer some pointers for writing your first assignment.

Read and explore the title

It is likely that your first written assignment will take the form of a given question or task. *'What ideas of God are found in the book of Genesis?'* or *'What is meant by mission? What model or models of mission have you observed in your placement church?'* A key part of the process is to examine carefully the title and any instructions given with it, such as suggested reading. If there are instructions about how the task is to be undertaken, read them carefully and think about the steps to be taken. Plan when you will do the reading or other research work and what you need to focus on to address the task. If there are no instructions, a way of tackling this stage is to examine the title by asking a number of questions. What are the key words in the title? Does the title have various parts to it? What is being asked in each part? Are key assessment words used, for example, *describe* or *evaluate*? What kind of information will I need to tackle this and where will I find it? For example, lecture notes, relevant books, placement journal, Internet sites, conversations. Time spent at this stage on getting the task clear is usually very beneficial, in that it helps focus both research and note taking (and will save time later on).

Plan the essay and your time to do it

If you have spent time on analysing the title you may well have a tentative outline or essay plan before you start the research phase. This will probably change as you gather the material together, but it will give you some direction and alert you to things to focus in on in your reading. Plan time into your timetable to do the work. Begin with the end. When is the deadline? This does not have to be when you finish. Deadlines are final submission dates. It is usually best to aim at an earlier date. This means that if things do not go according to plan or take longer, you have some leeway. When you have decided on the date by which you will be finished, work backwards planning in a date for a draft to be complete, time for writing and time for reading and gathering other information – and put them into your diary. Be as realistic as you can about the time needed, and then allow more time to be safe.

Research and take notes

The information you need may come from a variety of sources. Most commonly it will be found in books and articles, though it may also be from personal journals, interviews, visits or Internet sites. When you begin to gather your information you will need to take notes. People evolve their own ways of taking notes but if you are unsure how to start on this, you could use some of the following tools:

- *Read passages with questions in mind* even if they are simple ones, for example, what does the author say are key themes in John's Gospel?

- *Identify key sections, ideas, or paragraphs.* Some people underline passages books in pencil or pen. Clearly you should not do this unless the book is owned by you and you are happy for it to be marked, possibly permanently (remember you may read it again for a different purpose). You can tackle this in different ways, such as using Post-it notes, which you place on pages with your reminders. This allows you to continue the flow of the reading and return to the main passages later. Alternatively, you can make detailed notes on a piece of paper as you go, or brief notes referring to a page or paragraph to return to and make full notes, say, at the end of reading the chapter.

- *Organize your notes into meaningful structures,* perhaps using headings and numbered points. Identify and accurately copy any quotations you may want to use, but in the main write the notes in your own words rather than the words of the author. This helps you do the thinking work that creates understanding and also avoids unintentional plagiarism.

> **Plagiarism** is the **presentation of other persons' thoughts or writings as one's own. To avoid plagiarism you need to put ideas into your own words and indicate where you are quoting or using words or ideas drawn from other people.**

- *Revisit your notes* When you have completed all your research work, read them through and see what patterns or ideas seems to emerge and ask yourself questions. Is there anything I still don't grasp or have not got enough information about? Reread the title at this point to check whether your notes do relate to the assignment.

Make an essay plan

This is a key part of the work. Write the title at the top of the page, and then the section headings you will use to address the title. Under each section heading, make list of the points you want to make and think what conclusion this is leading towards. Ideally your essay plan will be on one side of A4 paper so you can see the structure under the title. Thus when you read through the plan, you can see whether it properly addresses the task. Remember that your essay is basically an argument or case to persuade the reader of the accuracy and truth of what you are saying. The points you make need to build up into a convincing and coherent presentation. When you read the headings, points and outline conclusion ask yourself: 'Does it directly address the task set?' and 'Is it convincing?' You should ask this at the plan stage so as to improve or strengthen your plan, and again when you have written the draft.

Prepare to write

Before you begin to write check the guidelines on presentation, referencing and bibliography. If you don't get this right, you will lose marks, even if your essay is good. Hence, it is sensible to use the required forms as you draft the essay and avoid having to spend a lot of time doing corrections later. If you are doing your writing on a word processor, this can be fairly easy if you adopt a discipline as you go. For example, put the word *Bibliography* or *References* on the first page and then make a page break before the word, so you have a page at the end where you can go to make a list of the books you have used. If you quote from a source or make reference to a source, list the source in full in the pattern required on the Bibliography page, and check in what form the reference should appear in the text or footnote. At the end of the writing you should have created your bibliography and references.

Write the assignment

When you are ready, write according to your plan, filling out each point under each heading and making sure there are good links between the paragraphs. Put in clear 'signposts'. These are ways of the telling the reader where you are going or where you have got to and what comes next. There are three points at which signposts are useful. First, at the beginning it is often helpful to tell the reader where you are going. For example, in the opening paragraph(s) you could say something like 'In order to answer the question, in this essay I shall first examine arguments for X, and then those against this view; I shall then consider the changing context of those involved in X in our society and indicate a way forward in my conclusion.' This tells people where you are going and will help them make sense of the structure and headings you use. The second point for a signpost is between sections or parts of the argument. For example, you might write, 'We have now looked at the key arguments for X, and although they appear strong we have identified key weak points. Let us now look at the arguments against X.' A third useful signpost is at the summary or conclusion where you are gathering the key strands of argument or case together. Here you might be saying something like 'In our examination of the main arguments for and against X, we concluded the arguments against were the more convincing and that the key arguments in favour were flawed. However, when considering the changing context of those involved in X, we see that the arguments cannot be settled without reference to Y because ... In this section we offer some tentative ideas for a way forward.'

Finalize and submit the assignment

When you have drafted the essay, read it through for sense, strength of argument and in order to correct typing or writing errors. Then set it aside for a day or two before rereading it. The value of this is that you read it again with fresh eyes and mind and may spot where the weak points are, where it needs to be clearer for the reader and whether the conclusion emerges out of the argument. Ask yourself again, 'Does it directly address the task set?' and 'Is it convincing?' Time spent at this point honing the essay is valuable. Read it aloud to yourself or ask someone else to read it and tell you, honestly, whether it makes sense and whether it addresses the task.

If you have a particular learning difficulty such as dyslexia, you may want to use a proofreader to make sure your writing is clear and spelling is accurate (word processor spelling checking is helpful but does not tell you when you have spelt the wrong word correctly or used the wrong form of a word which can be spelt differently (e.g., their/there or principle/principal)! The institution should have guidelines on what support is provided and what is appropriate and acceptable in preparing your work.

Going further

1. Look at the two essay titles given on page 188 above and think through the questions given for exploring titles. Even without the reading and

information you would need to answer these two questions, you can probably break the questions down into parts and identify the issues you would need to look into. See if you can make a simple plan of how to tackle each assignment.

2. Using the brief worked example we used of the pastoral carer, think about your future ministry and identify some of the ways you think it may be helpful for you to be assessed.

3. Read through the course handbooks for the programme you are to start.

    *   Identify the learning outcomes and write them out for yourself. Read through them several times, prayerfully, and keep the list somewhere to remind yourself of where you are headed.

    *   Have a look at the various assessment tasks in relation to different modules, units or parts of your course. What is each seeking to assess?

4. If you don't have a recent example, invest in a 'how to study' book. There are many small helpful books of this kind in student bookshops. The Open University's *The Good Study Guide* is one example, but there are many others.

Further reading

Stella Cottrell, *The Study Skills Handbook*, Macmillan, second edition, 2003.

Caroline Hall, *Getting Down to Writing: A Students' Guide to Overcoming Writer's Block*, Centre for Research into Human Communication, 1994.

Andy Northedge, *The Good Study Guide*, Open University, 2005.

15

Four pictures of Christian learning

We began this book by offering you a map, a simple overview of the process of learning and Christian formation as preparation for a recognized ministry. We end it by offering you the four great pictures of Christian growth and development which are present in the Scriptures as a way of drawing the book together.

The Bible speaks of most important themes not in long paragraphs of prose but in simple images. Over the whole development of the Scriptures, and particularly in the Gospels, these images provide ways of thinking about Christian formation: both our own growth and the way others around us may change and develop. They help us see different dimensions to what it means to grow as a disciple and a minister, and to see this growth as a lifetime's challenge. They need to be read alongside the insights on formation as God's work in Chapter 6.

The journey

The Bible is a book of journeys, from Genesis to Revelation. The Old Testament story in particular is shaped by two key journeys made by the people of Israel, both of which are full of meaning for the Church today. The first is the journey we know as the Exodus: the journey through the wilderness from slavery in Egypt to freedom in the Promised Land: a journey full of incident and adventure, as well as setbacks, learning and difficulties. From earliest times, the Church has seen the Exodus story as a picture and a place to learn about our own journey from captivity to freedom.

The second shaping journey in the Old Testament narrative is the journey into exile. After the destruction of Jerusalem in 587 BC, the people are taken into captivity in Babylon and long to return home. This return begins 70 years later and is seen by some of the prophets as a new Exodus. However, many Jews continued to live and be shaped by the experience of exile, something which has continued to the present day. Structures of faith, identity and community develop in exile which have tremendous power to sustain the people of God in difficult circumstances. In its own turn, the Christian Church has used the image of journeying through exile as a powerful picture of the calling of the Church until the return of Christ as king, and as a guide for how to live.

The journey images are echoed and deepened in the New Testament in the Gospel accounts both of the birth of Jesus (with a new journey down to Egypt and back) and also in the travelling of Jesus and the community of the first disciples. The earliest example of Christian community is not a static group in a single place but a community on the move. It is a community with purpose and a mission, a community whose members offer one another mutual support and learning, a place of teaching, dialogue and formation, and a community with a purpose, as Jesus' journey (actually called an exodus in Luke) moves ever closer to Jerusalem and to the cross.

It is perhaps not surprising that many of the best known of Jesus' parables are also set in the context of journeys: the travelling of a king to a far country, leaving his servants responsible for his house; the journey of a younger son away from his father and back again; the journey of a man going down from Jerusalem to Jericho. The longest and most striking of the resurrection stories is in the context of a journey out to Emmaus and back again.

The life of the early Church, according to Luke, is modelled on the life of Jesus and the disciples: small groups go out and make ever-longer journeys in order to carry the Christian gospel. One of the earliest descriptions of the followers of Jesus in Acts is as followers of 'The Way'. The writers of the New Testament letters make frequent use of the image of the race or the journey in the encouragement and teaching they offer in the Christian life. It is an image which is picked up and developed in Christian writing through the centuries (most notably in John Bunyan's allegory, *The Pilgrim's Progress*) and in hymns and songs in every generation ('Guide me O thou great redeemer, pilgrim through this barren land'; 'Will you come and follow me if I but call your name?').

This image of the journey is a helpful one to those who find themselves in a process of formation: you will find that you are moving on – sometimes literally, sometimes internally – in all kinds of ways. God will give you, in this part of the journey, new travelling companions and surprising mercy and grace. You may also find new landscapes: perhaps experiencing deserts as well as oases of rest along the way. Horizons will expand. Resources will be deepened.

Parenting and personal growth

The familiar language of God as father and mother is deeply embedded in the Old Testament traditions (Psalm 131; Hosea 11). It is of course developed by Jesus in profound ways in his teaching about the ways in which we pray, and in the story of the father and his two sons. The imagery is taken up in pictures of what happens when a person comes to faith in Christ: the change is so radical it is described in John's Gospel as being born again (or from above; John 3.3). Paul is particularly fond of this parenting picture to describe his relationship with the new Christians and churches. He describes himself as both a midwife and a mother in labour, encouraging those in his care to move on to greater maturity in Christ:

> And so, brothers and sisters, I could not speak to you as spiritual people, but rather as people of the flesh, as infants in Christ. I fed you with milk, not solid food, for you were not yet ready for solid food. (I Corinthians 3.2)

Christians are not born (or born again) fully formed and grown. There are processes of spiritual growth and development, maturity and regression which are not unlike our growth from infants to children to adolescents to adults. For the person who grows up in a Christian family and grows into faith as they grow older in years, these two processes may weave together in a very natural way. Your faith development may coincide very naturally with your life development. However, many people in Britain today (including many called to ministry) come to faith later in life. There is often a need, as there was with Nicodemus, to go back and learn some things all over again, like children, and a corresponding need to grow through dependence to maturity as adults in faith.

Significant and detailed work has been done in the last generation or so reflecting on how faith grows in children, young people and adults using this lens or image of growing to maturity, notably by a North American professor, James Fowler.[1] Those engaging in training for ministry will need to reflect on and understand this work, not only as a helpful tool in understanding their own development, but also as a way of ensuring that Christians in their care are able to grow to full Christian maturity. More recent studies on those who leave the Churches (by Alan Jameson and others) emphasize the need for continued growth in Christian maturity within communities of faith.[2]

Agricultural images

Both the Old and New Testaments were composed in largely agricultural societies. It should not surprise us, therefore, that many of the images for spiritual growth and discovery arise from the disciplines of growing crops and keeping animals. The Old Testament prophets speak of ploughing up the unploughed ground as a metaphor for the repentance required in a complacent society; of God planting Israel as a vineyard; of a harvest of righteousness; of God's care for the nation being like the tending of a flock of sheep.

Jesus takes all of these pictures and deepens them further with a particular focus on the bearing of fruit which is the aim of agriculture. The great parables of the kingdom feature seed and growth in abundance. The parable of the sower with its four kinds of soil illustrates the different obstacles and difficulties to Christian growth which are present throughout our Christian lives but especially at the beginning. The seed takes time to grow to maturity but can bear fruit a hundredfold. The image of the vine is much more an image of a tree in maturity where seasons of fruitfulness alternate with seasons of resting in the vine and of being pruned.

Paul uses the agricultural images to convey a sense of different roles in the task of ministry being assigned to different ministers, but says that the greatest part belongs to God:

> I planted. Apollos watered, but God gave the growth. So neither the one who plants nor the one who waters is anything, but only God who gives the growth. (1 Corinthians 3.6)

These agricultural images are particularly helpful reminders for Christian ministry in an industrial or post-industrial age. Most of our dominant thought patterns are metaphors taken from industrial production. We have therefore swallowed quite deeply the idea that Christian ministry can and should be continually productive, and that churches, like large companies, should be marked by strong and steady growth. When this does not happen (as is the case in every life and church), we feel that we ourselves (and sometimes other people) have failed in some way.

Fruitfulness is a much more helpful picture for Christian ministry than productivity or success. There is no single definition of fruitfulness in the Scriptures. Sometimes, quite clearly, the Bible speaks of the harvest as the number of people to be brought into the kingdom of God (Matthew 9.37-38). However, at other times fruitfulness is seen rather as practical outcomes (such as the justice and righteousness of Isaiah 5) or else personal qualities grown in our lives by the Spirit (Galatians 5.22). The agricultural metaphors carry the vital lessons of different forms of growth in different seasons in terms of spiritual growth and in terms of ministry. Seasons of rest and recovery alternate with seasons of fruitfulness over the pattern of a year and over the pattern of a lifetime. In turn, this can be a helpful picture for a period of training and formation: you may be called to step back for a time, to be less fruitful, in order to be prepared and deepened in your life and ministry for what is to come.

Building

The final great image used throughout Scripture for developing faith and ministry is that of building. Another central image in the life of the Old Testament community is that of the Temple set in the midst of Jerusalem, the city of God. The establishing of Jerusalem and the Temple is a sign of God's grace; their destruction a sign of God's judgement; their rebuilding a sign again of continued faithfulness. Concepts of foundations, measuring rods and steadfastness against attack are all used in the Psalms and elsewhere as powerful pictures of spiritual as well as physical qualities.

As with the other pictures, Jesus takes these images and develops them further. In the parable of the house builders, our whole life is seen to depend on the foundation on which we build. Paul continually encourages the Christian communities to build each other up in faith, strengthening the Church from its foundations. Once again, he uses the image to differentiate between the tasks of different builders: the foundations of faith are laid by someone else, but the responsibility for building ultimately rests with each individual believer:

> According to the grace of God given to me, like a skilled master builder I laid a foundation, and someone else is building on it. Each builder must choose with care how to build on it. For no one can lay any foundation other than the one that has been laid; that foundation is Jesus Christ.
> (1 Corinthians 3.10-11)

Read on a little further in this passage to discover that what is being built here is not just a little house but a temple – a temple of the Spirit – formed from the individual and community life of Christian people. It is a feature of building a temple or a great cathedral that the work is never finished: there is always development, refurbishment and improvement happening somewhere on the site.

Images and preparation for ministry

As you are called to ministry, so you are called to become, in the language of the journey, a better guide to others and one who equips them for their own pilgrimage. In the language of parenting, you are called to become a midwife, bringing new Christians to birth, and a spiritual parent allowing and encouraging disciples to grow beyond infancy to maturity and service in God's household. In the language of agriculture, you are called to be a shepherd, exercising leadership and guidance among the people of God; you are also called to plough, to sow, to weed and to prune so that God's people are fruitful in their season and are able to understand the dynamics of Christian life and ministry. Finally, in the language of Paul, you are called to become a skilled master builder, proficient in laying the foundation which is Jesus Christ but also able to teach others to build on that foundation for themselves so that the whole community is made stronger.

These callings are at the heart of what it means to be a Christian minister, however that ministry is exercised. They are also the key to understanding what it means to grow and be prepared for the exercise of this ministry: to become a better guide you need to move on yourself and to travel with many others; to become a better parent you need to face the challenges of your own growth and maturity; to become a better farmer you need to understand the rhythms of growth; what helps and what hinders; to become a better builder you need to work with and learn from those who have been apprenticed to that trade. Travelling and parenting, farming and building are rarely easy: they are demanding tasks but hugely fulfilling. There is great satisfaction in reaching the top of the mountain, in seeing a child grow to maturity, in planting and harvesting a crop, is seeing the end of a building project. In the same way learning for ministry is rarely easy, but as a lifelong enterprise it is hugely satisfying.

There is, then, much to learn for a demanding, complex and life-changing calling. May God bless you and enrich you as you move on in your own preparation for ministry and in your service of the gospel.

Notes

Chapter 5 Gifts, vocation and ministry

1   *Common Worship: Initiation Services*, Church House Publishing, 2000, p. 160.

2   *The Methodist Worship Book*, Methodist Publishing House, 1999, p. 290.

3   *The Methodist Worship Book*, p. 302.

4   The reference here is almost certainly to women deacons (like Phoebe) and not to the wives of the male deacons (as in some older translations).

5.   *The Methodist Worship Book*, p. 302.

Chapter 6 Understanding formation

1   We are indebted to Nicola Slee for some of the ideas that appear on pages 71–2 in a lecture she gave to the Methodist Conference, 2001.

2   Rule of Benedict, Preface 45–6, translated by Luke Dysinger.

Chapter 7 Balancing life

1   Gordon MacDonald, *Ordering Your Private World*, Highland, 1984, pp. 70–73. The book has a paragraph or so under each of these headings.

2   Alan Roxburgh, *The Missionary Congregation: Leadership and Liminality*, Trinity Press International, 1997, pp. 44–5.

Chapter 8 Learning in transition and community

1   Jean Vanier, *Community and Growth*, revised edition, Darton, Longman & Todd, 1989, pp. 330–31.

Chapter 11 Mission and ministry

1   Methodist Church, Minutes of the Conference, Methodist Publishing House, 2004, p. 1.

Chapter 12 Theological reflection

1   Donald A. Schön, *The Reflective Practitioner: How Professionals Think in Action*, Temple Smith, 1983.

2   Fr B. Hanley, *A Boy from Flanders*, YCW (not dated, circa 1985).

Chapter 13 Learning well

1   David Kolb, *Experiential Learning*, Prentice Hall, 1984.

2   Barbara Bruce, *7 Ways of Teaching the Bible to Children*, Abingdon, 1996; *7 Ways of Teaching the Bible to Adults*, Abingdon, 2000.

3   F. Marton and Säljö, 'On Qualitative Differences in Learning — 2: Outcome as a Function of the Learner's Conception of the Task', *British Journal of Educational Psychology* 46, 1967, pp. 115–27. Also see P. Ramsden, *Learning to Teach in Higher Education*, Routledge, 1992.

4   Jennifer A. Moon, *Reflection in Learning and Professional Development*, Kogan Page, 1999.

Chapter 15 Four pictures of Christian learning

1   James W. Fowler, *Becoming Christian: Adult Development and Christian Faith*, Harper & Row, 1984.

2   Alan Jameson, *A Churchless Faith*, SPCK, 2002.

General index

Note: Page references in *italics* indicate definitions

Index of biblical references

CPSIA information can be obtained at www.ICGtesting.com
Printed in the USA
LVOW06s1415290815

451954LV00001B/1/P